Journeys:

Communication
for the Global Age

Kouichi Ano
Norifumi Ueda
Michiko Toyama
Masataka Toshima
Takako Machimura
Karen Haedrich

Asahi Press

音声再生アプリ「リスニング・トレーナー」を使った音声ダウンロード

朝日出版社開発のアプリ、「リスニング・トレーナー（リストレ）」を使えば、教科書の音声をスマホ、タブレットに簡単にダウンロードできます。どうぞご活用ください。

◉ アプリ【リスニング・トレーナー】の使い方

《アプリのダウンロード》

App Store または Google Play から「リスニング・トレーナー」のアプリ（無料）をダウンロード

App Storeはこちら▶

Google Playはこちら▶

《アプリの使い方》

① アプリを開き「コンテンツを追加」をタップ
② 画面上部に【15704】を入力しDoneをタップ

音声ストリーミング配信 ≫≫≫

この教科書の音声は、右記ウェブサイトにて無料で配信しています。

https://text.asahipress.com/free/english/

表紙デザイン ：大下賢一郎
イラスト ：駿高泰子
執筆協力 ：石井真美

Journeys: Communication for the Global Age
Copyright © 2023 by Asahi Press

Preface

みなさんの英語学習の目的はどのようなものでしょうか？「英語という言葉が好き」「将来の仕事に必要だから」「海外旅行を楽しみたい」「世界中にたくさんの友達を作りたい」など人それぞれだと思います。でも、どんな目的であっても共通していること、それは「英語という窓」がみなさんの未来の可能性を広げてくれるということです。将来の夢を持っている人は、その夢に向かう Journey（旅）を英語がガイドしてくれます。まだ夢を探している人には、英語がみなさんのJourney を少しずつ先へと伸ばしていってくれることでしょう。このテキストは、大学生のみなさんがコミュニケーションのツールとして英語を使いこなし、夢を叶えるための支援をするために生まれました。Communication for the Global Age、グローバル社会で活躍するみなさんが、コミュニケーションのツールとしての英語力を伸ばしていくために、存分に活用してもらいたいと思っています。現代の社会はめまぐるしく変化をしています。時代で変わること、変わらないことを踏まえて、本書の改訂を行いました。新しい題材を取り入れるとともに、みなさんの英語の発信力を高めるためのRetellingなども新設しました。

英語を知識として終わらせるのではなく、活用できるスキルとして学習するために、それぞれの Lesson は 2 つの学習目標（CAN-DO）を軸として展開します。1 つは、大学生にとって身近で興味がある話題について考え、英語を通して視野を広げることを目指したものです。そしてもう 1 つは、Lesson の学習を通してみなさんが「英語でできるようになること」を具体的に表しています。学習を始める前にCAN-DOを確認しましょう。そして学習後には、どのくらいできるようになったかを CAN-DO Check で確認しながら、「英語でできること」を少しずつ増やしていきましょう。

それでは、アメリカに留学をして様々な異文化体験を重ねる日本人大学生の春樹、そして将来の夢に向かって前向きに大学生活を送るアメリカ人女子学生のKatie といっしょに、Journeys を楽しみましょう。

阿野　幸一

Contents

はじめに
本書の使い方

本書の使い方

> ## Conversation
>
> レッスンのテーマに沿った話題について、Katie と春樹の 2 人が会話を行っています。大学生同士の生き生きとした会話から、自然な会話の流れを学習します。詳しい情報をつかむ前に、2 人の会話の流れをつかみ、その後に、内容についての先生からの質問に答えたり、リズムやイントネーションなどに注意をしたりしながら音読練習や役割練習を行いましょう。

> ## CAN-DO
>
> これから学習するレッスンのゴール（英語の学習を通してできるようになること）を、学習の開始前に確認し、目指すべきゴールを明確にします。それぞれのレッスンに 2 つの CAN-DO を示しています。題材を通して考えて理解する目標と、レッスンで学習する言語材料を通して表現できるようになる目標の 2 つです。

Lesson 1 Communication

CAN-DO

☑ コミュニケーションが持つ力について理解することができる。

☑ 相手のことを考えて自分のことを紹介することができる。

Warm-up Questions – Talk in pairs!

1. Can you name three forms of communication?
2. Which do you like better, face-to-face communication or social network communication?

Keywords

facial expressions
gestures
dancing … art … non-verbal … verbal
paintings

Communication

oral
written
face-to-face conversations
radio programs
YouTube
letters
blogs

Conversation

Haruki is a student from Japan studying at a college in Boston, Massachusetts, U.S.A. He is talking to his friend Katie as they take a walk on the college campus.

1-02

Katie: Haruki, what made you interested in studying English?

Haruki: Well, since I was little, I have always loved baseball.

Katie: Baseball?

Haruki: Yes. My favorite player played for a team in the United States.

Katie: I see.

Haruki: I saw the faces of fans like me in the crowd. I knew that if we could talk to each other, we would have so many interesting stories to tell!

Katie: I get it. You wanted to make friends who shared your love of baseball!

Haruki: That's right.

Useful Expressions

I see.
I get it.
That's right.

Pronunciation

ポーズを見つける＝情報・意味のまとまりごとに聞く

ポーズとは「音の切れ目」です。会話を聞きながら、ポーズを探しましょう。例えば会話の 1 行目では、Haruki, / what made you interested in studying English? のように、Haruki と呼びかけ、質問に入る前にポーズを入れています。人が話す時は、まとまった情報（あるいは意味）の切れ目にポーズを入れるため、英語を聞く時にポーズを意識して聞くトレーニングは、情報のまとまりごとに聞いて理解し、次の情報に備える力を伸ばしてくれます。

Let's Try!

1. 会話を聞いてポーズの箇所に／を入れましょう。
1-02
2. ポーズで区切られた意味のまとまりを意識して話す練習をしましょう。
1-03
3. 電話番号を聞いて、a と b のどちらかに丸をつけてみましょう。
   a. 046-732-2885　or　b. 0467-322-885
   ペアになって正しく伝えられるか確認してみましょう。

> **写真（2つ）** 写真を通して、題材へのイメージを膨らませます。この写真を用いて、みなさんが思い浮かべることを伝えたり、クラスメートとやり取りをしたりします。

> ## Warm-up Questions – Talk in pairs!
>
> 2 つの質問についてみなさんが自分の答えを考えて用意し、ペアになって話し合うことで、授業で英語を使う準備をするとともに、題材について考えるきっかけとします。ペアを変えながらやり取りを繰り返すことで、次第に英語で話すことに慣れていきます。

> ## Keywords
>
> 題材理解を深めるためのキーワードです。"Warm-up Questions – Talk in pairs!" の際に活用することができます。また、ペアワークを終えたあとで、英語による表現力を高めるための語彙の補強として利用することもできます。

> ## Useful Expressions
>
> Conversation の中から、日常会話でよく使われる表現を 3 つ取り上げています。みなさんに日常会話で使えるようになってもらいたい表現なので、どのような場面で使われているかを考え、自分でも使えるように練習して実際に使ってみましょう。

Reading

My name is Janet Smith. I was born in a small town in *Maine, on the east coast of the United States. Today, I am going to talk about the way that "communication" has affected me in my experience with Japanese language and culture. From the first time that I heard spoken Japanese, I aspired to be able to understand the messages that were being communicated and to be able to tell my story as well. 5

I became interested in Japanese culture in high school. Japanese media was becoming popular in the United States at that time. I saw Japanese anime on TV and Japanese manga in bookstores. However, it was almost always translated into English. I remember when I rented an anime series on DVD and listened to the Japanese language soundtrack for the first time. 10 I had no idea what was being said, but I loved the sounds of the words. Written Japanese words looked complicated and beautiful. I longed to know what the words meant, but I didn't know anyone who spoke Japanese in my small town in Maine. 15

Little by little, I started listening to Japanese music. I knew that each lyric had a message for me. I also watched *clips from Japanese TV shows on the Internet. Each interview and conversation had a story to tell. If I could understand the words, I would come to know more about the world that those words came from. 20

I began to study Japanese language at college in Boston a few years later. I finally had a chance to come to Tokyo for the first time in my *sophomore year of college. I stepped off the plane at Narita Airport. For the first time, outside of my classroom or a recording on a CD, I heard people all around me speaking in native Japanese. 25

Stepping into a new culture was exciting and enchanting, but also unfamiliar and overwhelming. Clutching a map, I built up my courage to ask a woman for directions on the street. When I asked my question in Japanese, the woman listened thoughtfully, gave me an answer, and pointed in the direction that I should go. 30

It was a simple exchange, but I was thrilled when I was understood. It was as if I had found a secret code. "Communication" was the tool that had unlocked a new world for me. This world was full of people with stories to tell. Now, with the power of communication, I had a way to listen to their stories and learn more about this new world. 35

Vocabulary
Maine：アメリカ合衆国の最東北部に位置する州　clip(s)：動画の1カット
years of college：freshman（大学1年生）、sophomore（大学2年生）、junior（大学3年生）、senior（大学4年生）

Comprehension
Read the passage, and fill in the table below.
Janet のスピーチの要点を、以下の表に英語で書いてみましょう。

スピーチのテーマ	The way that "communication" has affected Janet in her experience with Japanese language and culture.
日本文化に興味を持ったきっかけ	Janet saw Japanese anime on TV and Japanese manga in bookstores.
DVD や CD で初めて日本語を聞いた時の感想	
日本語を聞き続けての感想	
大学時代にした経験	
初めて日本語で会話した時の感想	
ジャネットにとってのコミュニケーションの定義とは	

Lesson 1

Communication

4

5

Reading の題材について、皆さんの考えを述べるための質問です。一つの正解はありません。みなさんが考えたことを、自由に英語で表現してみましょう。ペアやグループになって、ディスカッションをして、お互いの意見を聞き、自分の考えも述べたり、相手に質問をしたりしてみましょう。

Retelling

Reading で読んだ本文の中から、ポイントとなる部分に焦点を当てて、英文の内容を自分の英語で再生していく表現活動です。イラストやキーワードを参考にして内容を伝えることで、英語による発信力を向上させます。

Answer the Questions

Work with a partner to answer the questions. Use complete sentences.

1. When Janet listened to Japanese for the first time, how did she feel?

2. What did the Japanese shows on the Internet make Janet think?

3. What is the definition of the word "communication" for Janet?

Discussion Topic

What does the word "communication" mean to you?

Retelling

イラストとキーワードを使って、筆者 (Janet) はコミュニケーションとはどのようなものだと述べているか、書き出しの英語 (According to Janet,) に続くように英語で説明しなさい。また、本文の内容を参考に、あなた自身が考えるコミュニケーションについて英語で説明してみましょう。

"Communication" = the tool　unlock　a new world

Janet

full / people / stories / tell

Grammar for Communication

▶ 【現在にかかわることを述べる表現：現在形・現在進行形】
1-10

◆ 現在形：現在の動作や状態、習慣的な事実などを表す。
例文：
I am a first-year economics student. （私は経済学を学んでいる1年生です。）
I take a walk every day. （私は毎日散歩します。）

◆ 現在進行形：話をしている時点で進行している動作を述べる。
The girl is drawing a dog in her sketchbook now.
（その少女は今スケッチブックに犬を書いています。）

＊状態を表す動詞は、進行形にならないものがあることに注意しましょう。

★動画で分かる！
文法解説

Let's Try!

場面に合うようにカッコ内の動詞を適切な形に変え、空所を埋めて英文を完成させましょう。

1. A: Where is Jim?

   B: He _____ out at the moment. (be)

2. A: Hello. May I speak to Marina?

   B: May I ask who _____? (call)

3. Kim _____ her mother very much. (resemble)

4. Hi, I'm Kento. I _____ climate change at the institute now. (study)

5. My father _____ a bike for commuting. (ride)

Lesson 1

Communication

Grammar for Communication

高校までに知識として学習してきた英文法を、コミュニケーションに使える文法力に転化させるための学習コーナーです。言葉の使用場面と働きを意識したテーマを設定し、複数の文法事項を関連させ、比較しながら、文法知識の整理を行います。
Let's Try! の練習問題を通して知識の確認を図りますが、みなさん自身のことに置き換えて表現することで、文法をより身近に感じる練習にすることができます。

★代表著者による文法解説動画

各 Lesson の文法事項を動画で詳しく解説しています。文法の使い方について、解説動画を通して学習し、コミュニケーションで活用できる文法力を身につけましょう。

●動画ストリーミングサイト
トップページへ

Journeys
Communication for the Global Age
文法解説

Express Yourself

このコーナーでは、どのように英語で表現をするのが効果的かについて学習し、みなさんの英語による発信力を高めます。単に知識としての学習で終わらせないために、Speaking Task で実際に英語で話す練習をします。また、Writing Task では、英文をつなげてパラグラフを構成していく練習も行います。英語の発信力を高めるために、実際に話したり書いたりすることがとても大切です。

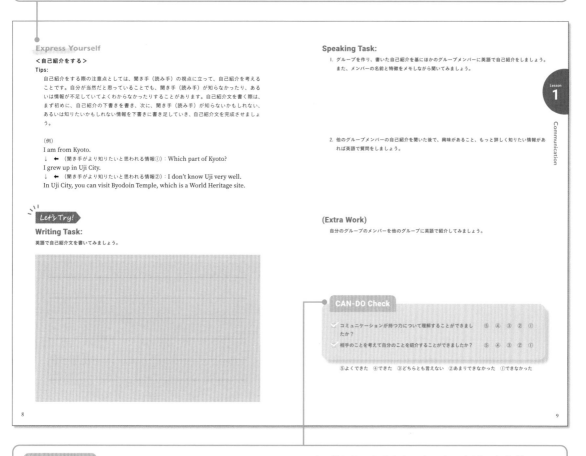

Express Yourself

＜自己紹介をする＞
Tips:
自己紹介をする際の注意点としては、聞き手（読み手）の視点に立って、自己紹介を考えることです。自分が当然だと思っていることでも、聞き手（読み手）が知らなかったり、あるいは情報が不足していてよくわからなかったりすることがあります。自己紹介を書く際は、まず初めに、自己紹介の下書きを書き、次に、聞き手（読み手）が知らないかもしれない、あるいは知りたいかもしれない情報を下書きに書き足していき、自己紹介文を完成させましょう。

（例）
I am from Kyoto.
↓ ◀ （聞き手がより知りたいと思われる情報①）: Which part of Kyoto?
I grew up in Uji City.
↓ ◀ （聞き手がより知りたいと思われる情報②）: I don't know Uji very well.
In Uji City, you can visit Byodoin Temple, which is a World Heritage site.

Let's Try!
Writing Task:
英語で自己紹介文を書いてみましょう。

Speaking Task:
1. グループを作り、書いた自己紹介を基にほかのグループメンバーに英語で自己紹介をしましょう。また、メンバーの名前と特徴をメモしながら聞いてみましょう。

2. 他のグループメンバーの自己紹介を聞いた後で、興味があること、もっと詳しく知りたい情報があれば英語で質問をしましょう。

(Extra Work)
自分のグループのメンバーを他のグループに英語で紹介してみましょう。

CAN-DO Check
☑ コミュニケーションが持つ力について理解することができましたか？　⑤　④　③　②　①
☑ 相手のことを考えて自分のことを紹介することができましたか？　⑤　④　③　②　①

⑤よくできた　④できた　③どちらとも言えない　②あまりできなかった　①できなかった

Lesson 1
Communication

8

9

CAN-DO Check

単元での学習の振り返りを行うコーナーです。みなさん自身が、学習前と学習後でどのくらい変化したかを振り返ります。ポイントは「できるかできないか」ではなく「どのくらいできるようになったか」ということです。「よくできるようになった」と思ったら⑤にマークを、「まだできない」と思ったら①にマークというように5段階で確認します。ここではクラスメートとの比較ではなく、自分自身の変化を確認することが大切です。

Journeys:

Communication
for the Global Age

Asahi Press

CAN-DO

☑ コミュニケーションが持つ力について理解することができる。

☑ 相手のことを考えて自分のことを紹介することができる。

Warm-up Questions – Talk in pairs!

1. Can you name three forms of communication?

2. Which do you like better, face-to-face communication or social network communication?

Keywords

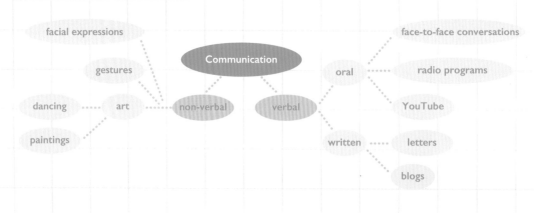

Conversation

Haruki is a student from Japan studying at a college in Boston, Massachusetts, U.S.A. He is talking to his friend Katie as they take a walk on the college campus.

Katie: Haruki, what made you interested in studying English?

Haruki: Well, since I was little, I have always loved baseball.

Katie: Baseball?

Haruki: Yes. My favorite player played for a team in the United States.

Katie: I see.

Haruki: I saw the faces of fans like me in the crowd. I knew that if we could talk to each other, we would have so many interesting stories to tell!

Katie: I get it. You wanted to make friends who shared your love of baseball!

Haruki: That's right.

Useful Expressions

I see.

I get it.

That's right.

Pronunciation

ポーズを見つける＝情報・意味のまとまりごとに聞く

ポーズとは「音の切れ目」です。会話を聞きながら、ポーズを探しましょう。例えば会話の1行目では、Haruki, / what made you interested in studying English? のように、Haruki と呼びかけ、質問に入る前にポーズを入れています。人が話す時は、まとまった情報（あるいは意味）の切れ目にポーズを入れるため、英語を聞く時にポーズを意識して聞くトレーニングは、情報のまとまりごとに聞いて理解し、次の情報に備える 力を伸ばしてくれます。

Let's Try!

1. 会話を聞いてポーズの箇所に／を入れましょう。

2. ポーズで区切られた意味のまとまりを意識して話す練習をしましょう。

3. 電話番号を聞いて、a と b のどちらかに丸をつけてみましょう。

    a. 046-732-2885　or　b. 0467-322-885

ペアになって正しく伝えられるか確認してみましょう。

3

Reading

1-04
My name is Janet Smith. I was born in a small town in *Maine, on the east coast of the United States. Today, I am going to talk about the way that "communication" has affected me in my experience with Japanese language and culture. From the first time that I heard spoken Japanese, I aspired to be able to understand the messages that were being communicated and to 5
be able to tell my story as well.

1-05
I became interested in Japanese culture in high school. Japanese media was becoming popular in the United States at that time. I saw Japanese anime on TV and Japanese manga in bookstores. However, it was almost always translated into English. I remember when I rented an anime series 10
on DVD and listened to the Japanese language soundtrack for the first time. I had no idea what was being said, but I loved the sounds of the words. Written Japanese words looked complicated and beautiful. I longed to know what the words meant, but I didn't know anyone who spoke Japanese in my small town in Maine. 15

1-06
Little by little, I started listening to Japanese music. I knew that each lyric had a message for me. I also watched *clips from Japanese TV shows on the Internet. Each interview and conversation had a story to tell. If I could understand the words, I would come to know more about the world that those words came from. 20

1-07
I began to study Japanese language at college in Boston a few years later. I finally had a chance to come to Tokyo for the first time in my *sophomore year of college. I stepped off the plane at Narita Airport. For the first time, outside of my classroom or a recording on a CD, I heard people all around me speaking in native Japanese. 25

1-08

Stepping into a new culture was exciting and enchanting, but also unfamiliar and overwhelming. Clutching a map, I built up my courage to ask a woman for directions on the street. When I asked my question in Japanese, the woman listened thoughtfully, gave me an answer, and pointed in the direction that I should go. ₃₀

1-09

It was a simple exchange, but I was thrilled when I was understood. It was as if I had found a secret code. "Communication" was the tool that had unlocked a new world for me. This world was full of people with stories to tell. Now, with the power of communication, I had a way to listen to their stories and learn more about this new world. ₃₅

Lesson **1**

Communication

Vocabulary

Maine：アメリカ合衆国の最東北部に位置する州　**clip(s)**：動画の 1 カット
years of college：**freshman**（大学 1 年生）、**sophomore**（大学 2 年生）、**junior**（大学 3 年生）、**senior**（大学 4 年生）

Comprehension

Read the passage, and fill in the table below.
Janet のスピーチの要点を、以下の表に英語で書いてみましょう。

スピーチのテーマ	The way that "communication" has affected Janet in her experience with Japanese language and culture.
日本文化に興味を持ったきっかけ	Janet saw Japanese anime on TV and Japanese manga in bookstores.
DVD や CD で初めて日本語を聞いた時の感想	
日本語を聞き続けての感想	
大学時代にした経験	
初めて日本語で会話した時の感想	
ジャネットにとってのコミュニケーションの定義とは	

5

Answer the Questions

Work with a partner to answer the questions. Use complete sentences.

1. When Janet listened to Japanese for the first time, how did she feel?

   ....

2. What did the Japanese shows on the Internet make Janet think?

   ....

3. What is the definition of the word "communication" for Janet?

   ....

Discussion Topic

What does the word
"communication" mean
to you?

Retelling

イラストとキーワードを使って、筆者（Janet）はコミュニケーションとはどのようなもだと述べているか、書き出しの英語（According to Janet,）に続くように英語で説明しなさい。また、本文の内容を参考に、あなた自身が考えるコミュニケーションについて英語で説明してみましょう。

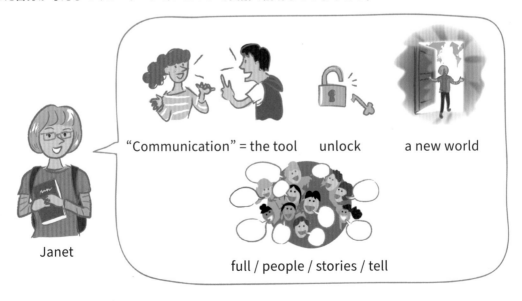

Janet

"Communication" = the tool   unlock   a new world

full / people / stories / tell

Grammar for Communication

▶ 【現在にかかわることを述べる表現：現在形・現在進行形】

1-10 ◆ 現在形：現在の動作や状態、習慣的な事実などを表す。

例文：

I am a first-year economics student. （私は経済学を学んでいる1年生です。）

I take a walk every day. （私は毎日散歩します。）

◆ 現在進行形：話をしている時点で進行している動作を述べる。

The girl is drawing a dog in her sketchbook now.

（その少女は今スケッチブックに犬を書いています。）

★動画で分かる！
文法解説

＊状態を表す動詞は、進行形にならないものがあることに注意しましょう。

Lesson
1

Communication

Let's Try!

場面に合うようにカッコ内の動詞を適切な形に変え、空所を埋めて英文を完成させましょう。

1. A: Where is Jim?

   B: He _____ out at the moment. (be)

2. A: Hello. May I speak to Marina?

   B: May I ask who _____? (call)

3. Kim _____ her mother very much. (resemble)

4. Hi, I'm Kento. I _____ climate change at the institute now. (study)

5. My father _____ a bike for commuting. (ride)

Express Yourself

＜自己紹介をする＞

Tips:

自己紹介をする際の注意点としては、聞き手（読み手）の視点に立って、自己紹介を考えることです。自分が当然だと思っていることでも、聞き手（読み手）が知らなかったり、あるいは情報が不足していてよくわからなかったりすることがあります。自己紹介文を書く際は、まず初めに、自己紹介の下書きを書き、次に、聞き手（読み手）が知らないかもしれない、あるいは知りたいかもしれない情報を下書きに書き足していき、自己紹介文を完成させましょう。

（例）

I am from Kyoto.

↓　　←　（聞き手がより知りたいと思われる情報①）：Which part of Kyoto?

I grew up in Uji City.

↓　　←　（聞き手がより知りたいと思われる情報②）：I don't know Uji very well.

In Uji City, you can visit Byodoin Temple, which is a World Heritage site.

Writing Task:

英語で自己紹介文を書いてみましょう。

Speaking Task:

1. グループを作り、書いた自己紹介を基にほかのグループメンバーに英語で自己紹介をしましょう。
また、メンバーの名前と特徴をメモしながら聞いてみましょう。

2. 他のグループメンバーの自己紹介を聞いた後で、興味があること、もっと詳しく知りたい情報があれば英語で質問をしましょう。

(Extra Work)

自分のグループのメンバーを他のグループに英語で紹介してみましょう。

CAN-DO Check

☑ コミュニケーションが持つ力について理解することができましたか？ ⑤ ④ ③ ② ①

☑ 相手のことを考えて自分のことを紹介することができましたか？ ⑤ ④ ③ ② ①

⑤よくできた　④できた　③どちらとも言えない　②あまりできなかった　①できなかった

Lesson 2 Friendship

CAN-DO

- ☑ 友情のいろいろな形について理解することができる。
- ☑ 過去の出来事について説明することができる。

Warm-up Questions – Talk in pairs!

1. Can you describe your best friend? Why do you like him/her?

2. What are friends for?

Keywords

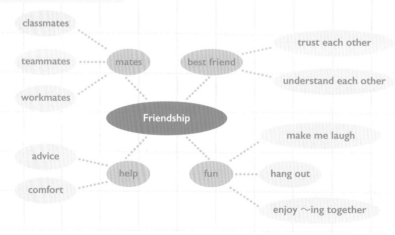

classmates

teammates ..... mates — best friend — trust each other

workmates — understand each other

Friendship

make me laugh

advice

help — fun ..... hang out

comfort

enjoy ～ing together

Conversation

Katie took a trip to New York City last weekend. She gives her friend Haruki a keychain that she bought for him there.

1-11

Katie: Here, Haruki, I have a present for you.

Haruki: For me? It's a keychain! Thanks, Katie.

Katie: I bought it when I was in New York City last weekend.

Haruki: How was the Big Apple?

Katie: It was fun! I even learned some history. Did you know that the Statue of Liberty was a gift of friendship from France to the United States?

Haruki: No, I didn't know that. I guess countries can be friends, just like people!

Katie: Sure!

Useful Expressions

Here.

How was...?

Sure!

Pronunciation

際立った語を見つける＝大切な言葉を拾いながら聞く

それぞれの情報のまとまりには、他より際立った語（の一部）があります。他と比べてハッキリ／高く／長く聞こえる語は、それが重要である印です。例えば、会話の 1 行目の文で際立っている語は "present" です。英語を聞いて理解するためには、「際立った語＝重要な語」に敏感な耳をつくる練習が必要です。

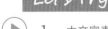

1. 大文字表記された際立った語（の一部）を意識して、会話の冒頭を聞きましょう。

1-12
Here, Haruki, I have a PREsent for you.
For ME? It's a KEYchain! THANKS, Katie.
I BOUGHT it when I was in NEW YORK City last weekend.

2. 会話の残りを聞いて、際立った語に下線を引き、ペアで答え合わせをしましょう。

1-13

Reading

1-14

On March 27th, 1912, Yukio Ozaki, the mayor of Tokyo, gave a gift of friendship to the American city of Washington, D.C.: more than 3,000 Japanese cherry trees. Now, an event called the National Cherry Blossom Festival is held every spring in Washington, D.C. to celebrate the lasting friendship between the two countries.   5

1-15

The first National Cherry Blossom Festival was held in 1935. In 2012, on the 100th anniversary of the gift, there was a *centennial celebration in the form of a special five-week festival. Every year, the festival begins in late March, around the time when the cherry blossoms are most likely to bloom, and lasts for several weeks. Thousands of blooming cherry trees   10 can be seen around the *Tidal Basin in West Potomac Park, in East Potomac Park, and on the grounds of the Washington Monument.

1-16

Some notable annual events include the opening ceremony, the Southwest Waterfront fireworks display, and the National Cherry Blossom Festival Parade. Other events include cultural activities, such as art   15 exhibits, music and dance performances, fashion shows, and marching bands. Reportedly, more than a million people visit Washington each year to view the blossoms.

1-17

After the initial planting of the cherry trees in 1912, Japan and the United States continued to give each other gifts as signs of goodwill. In   20 1915, the United States gave a gift of flowering dogwood trees to the people of Japan. In 1954, in order to commemorate the signing of the 1854 *Japan-U.S. Treaty of Amity and Friendship, a 300-year-old stone lantern was given to the city of Washington by the Japanese ambassador, Sadao Iguchi. The lantern is ceremonially lit once a year during the festival.   25

1-18

The annual National Cherry Blossom Festival in Washington, D.C. serves as an important reminder of the international friendship and goodwill between Japan and the United States. The festival celebrates both Japanese and American culture, as well as the close relationship between the two countries. People from around the world can appreciate this friendship by remembering the gift of the beautiful cherry trees. 30

Vocabulary

centennial：100 周年の　Tidal Basin：アメリカ合衆国ワシントン D.C. のナショナル・モールの南側に位置し、ポトマック川に隣接する入り江　Japan-U.S. Treaty of Amity and Friendship：日米和親条約（1854 年 3 月 31 日に江戸幕府とアメリカ合衆国が締結した条約）

Comprehension

Read the passage, and fill in the table below.

1. 日米友好の贈り物について、以下の年表にまとめてみましょう。

Year	A gift of friendship	
	from Japan to the U.S.	from the U.S. to Japan
1912	more than 3,000 Japanese cherry trees	
1915		
1954		

2. アメリカ合衆国の首都ワシントン D.C. で毎年行われている「桜祭り」について、以下の表にまとめてみましょう。

The annual National Cherry Blossom Festival	
始まり	The first National Cherry Blossom Festival was held in 1935.
開催地	
開催時期	
開催期間	
桜が植樹されている場所	
イベントの内容	
桜祭りの役割	
2012 年に行われたこと	

Answer the Questions

Work with a partner to answer the questions. Use complete sentences.

1. Why is the National Cherry Blossom Festival held?

    ....

2. What are some notable events that the festival has every year?

    ....

3. What was the gift that the Japanese ambassador gave to the city of Washington in 1954?

    ....

4. What does the annual National Cherry Blossom Festival remind us of?

    ....

Discussion Topic

What do you have to do
in order to keep good
"friendship"?

Retelling

次の英文の書き出しと終わりの文につながるように、表中のキーワードとイラストを使って、日米友好の贈り物について英語で説明しましょう。

In order to commemorate the signing of the 1854 Japan-U.S. Treaty of Amity and Friendship, _____.

Year	A gift of friendship 🎁	
1912	Japan 🎁→ U.S. ⚫ 🇺🇸	Yukio Ozaki, the mayor of Tokyo 🎁↓ more than 3,000 Japanese cherry trees the American city of Washington, D.C.
1915	U.S. 🇺🇸 🎁→ Japan ⚫	the United States 🎁↓ a gift of flowering dogwood trees the people of Japan
1954	Japan ⚫ 🎁→ U.S. 🇺🇸	the Japanese ambassador, Sadao Iguchi 🎁↓ a 300-year-old stone lantern the city of Washington

The lantern is ceremonially lit once a year during the festival.

Grammar for Communication

1-19

【過去のことを述べる表現：過去形・過去進行形】

◆ 過去形：過去の動作や状態、過去における事実などを表します。

I started listening to American music. （私はアメリカの音楽を聴き始めました。）

◆ 過去進行形：過去のある時点で進行していた動作を述べます。

K-pop music was becoming popular in Thailand when I went there.

（私がタイを訪れたとき、K-pop 音楽は現地で人気になりつつありました。）

★動画で分かる！
文法解説

Let's Try!

カッコ内の動詞を適切な形に変え、空所を埋めて英文を完成させましょう。

When I (1)_____(be) a child, my father (2)_____(show) me a video about animals. The video (3)_____(make) me so excited that I (4)_____(not get) tired of it. Around that time, I (5)_____(dream) of visiting Africa to see the animals on the savanna.

Express Yourself

＜過去の出来事を説明する＞

Tips:

- ◆ 過去の出来事を説明する際には、いつ (when)、どこで (where)、なにが (what)、どのように（how）起こったか、またその結果どのようになったか (result) を、物事が起きた時間軸に沿って説明します。
- ◆ 過去の出来事を説明する際の時制は過去形を使いましょう。

Writing Task:

身近に起こった出来事で忘れられない思い出について説明する文章を英語で書きましょう。

(An Unforgettable Memory とはじめにタイトルをつけてから書き始めましょう。)

Speaking Task:

1. あなたの身近に起こった出来事で、忘れられない思い出について英語でグループのメンバーに発表しましょう。それぞれの発表中は話の要点をメモに取り、発表が終わったら、他のグループメンバーは発表に対する質問やコメントを英語でしましょう。

2. 他のグループメンバーの話の内容について、メモをもとにクラスに英語で発表しましょう。

CAN-DO Check

☑ 友情のいろいろな形について理解することができましたか？   ⑤ ④ ③ ② ①

☑ 過去の出来事について説明することができましたか？   ⑤ ④ ③ ② ①

Health and Environment

☑ 私たちの生活における水の大切さと安全な水の確保について理解し考えることができる。

☑ 自分の経験を伝えることができる。

SDGs

Sustainable
Development
Goals

Warm-up Questions – Talk in pairs!

1. What are three important natural resources?

2. What do you use water for every day?

Keywords

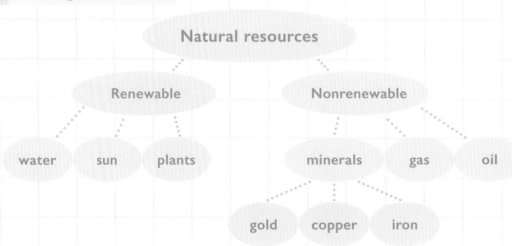

Conversation

Katie and Haruki have just finished eating some cake that Katie bought this afternoon. Haruki is washing the dishes.

Katie: Thanks for washing the dishes.

Haruki: No problem! The cake you brought was delicious. Which bakery did you go to?

Katie: The one near the movie theater. Hey, Haruki. You should turn off the water when you're not using it.

Haruki: Oh? Right. Sorry about that.

Katie: Don't you know about Goal 6 of the SDGs?

Haruki: What's that?

Katie: You should look it up online. You can also find good advice about how to save water.

Haruki: OK, I will!

Useful Expressions

Thanks for ....
No problem!
Sorry about that.

Pronunciation

イントネーション I

イントネーション（抑揚）とは、声の上げ下げを用いて意味の切れ目や、強調したい点、心情などの情報を伝える手段です。例えば会話の最後にある "OK, I will!" では、will で声の上下が際立っており、春樹の意欲的な様子（SDGs や節水方法について知りたい！）が伝わってきます。

Let's Try!

1. Useful expressions の抑揚を意識して会話練習をしましょう。

2. Katie が You should turn off the water when you're not using it. と言う時に、声を上下させ意味の切れ目を伝えています。どこでどのように上下しているか聞き、話し合いましょう。

19

Reading

1-21

Hi, everybody! My name is Abigail Johnson. I'm from Canada, and I'm a junior in college majoring in *environmental studies. Recently, I started this blog to write about topics that I find interesting. I also hope to inspire other people, especially college students like me, to think about important issues. 5

1-22

Today, I want to share my daily routine with you. Here it is. In the morning, I get up and brush my teeth, and then take a shower. After having breakfast at my kitchen table, I wash the dishes. Every weekend, I do my laundry. Sometimes I go to the gym, and I always *bring a refreshing bottle of water to stay hydrated. Maybe this sounds similar to your routine. I 10 realized that I take something for granted almost every day: access to safe, clean water.

1-23

I started researching this topic when I wrote a report about Goal 6 of the Sustainable Development Goals, or SDGs: "Ensure access to water and *sanitation for all." People are acutely aware of the importance of *hygiene 15 to prevent the spread of disease (for example, washing your hands). However, billions of people worldwide do not have access to safe drinking water or basic sanitation services, such as toilets.

1-24

Of course, this drastically affects people's health and quality of life. Every year, thousands of children die from *preventable diseases because their 20 families do not have access to clean water. India is the second-most populous country in the world, with 1.39 billion people, but recent data shows that only one in every five households has access to *piped water connections. Especially in rural areas, many people do not have water available inside their homes. When water is available, it is often contaminated. 25

Lack of access to water also keeps communities in poverty. For example, in some areas of Sub-Saharan Africa, people have to walk long distances to retrieve water. This is usually done by women and children. Plastic containers of water are extremely heavy, and this difficult task takes a lot of time and effort. So, women and children cannot spend their time on education or other activities. Education is necessary to lift communities out of poverty. Imagine how different their lives would be if they could just turn on the tap in their home to get water! As you can see, access to water affects these communities in many ways.

Luckily, there is a solution. Actually, many solutions! People are thinking of creative and innovative ways to bring clean water to these areas that desperately need it. There are organizations such as the Water Project and the Tap Project working on these issues. For example, they build wells and pumps in convenient locations so people don't have to travel far for their water. Another program called the WATERSPOUTT project researched and developed solar water disinfection technology called SODIS. There are also devices for safely collecting and storing rainwater. Personally, I can't wait to see the next innovative solution to solve the water crisis. Who knows? Maybe you'll be the one to think of it!

Vocabulary

environmental studies：環境学　(bring) a refreshing bottle of water to stay hydrated：水分補給のために清涼飲料水をボトル（で持っていく）　sanitation：（公衆）衛生　hygiene：（個人の身体の）衛生　preventable disease(s)：予防可能な病気　piped water：水道

Comprehension

Read the passage, and fill in the table below.
本文の内容を以下の表にまとめましょう。

(1)安全で清潔な水を利用できる人の生活の一例

Abigail Johnson's Daily Routine	
in the morning	get up / brush her teeth / take a shower
after having breakfast	wash the (　　　　　)
every weekend	do her (　　　　　)
sometimes / always	go to the gym / bring a refreshing bottle of (　　　　　) to stay hydrated

(2)安全で清潔な水を利用できない人々の状況

Lack of access to safe drinking water or basic sanitation services			
People's health and quality of life	Thousands of children (　　　　) from (　　　　) diseases.		
	Lack of access to water keeps communities in (　　　　).		
	Women and children cannot spend their time on (　　　　) or other activities.		

Answer the Questions

Work with a partner to answer the questions. Use complete sentences.

1. What are two reasons for Abigail Johnson to write the blog?

   ....

2. What does "SDGs" stand for?

   ....

3. What is Goal 6 of the SDGs?

   ....

4. What is needed for people's good health and quality of life?

   ....

5. If women and children didn't have to walk long distances to retrieve water, what could they spend their time on?

   ....

Discussion Topic

How can we solve Goal 6
of the SDGs?

22

Retelling

次のキーワードを参考に、「安全で清潔な水を利用できない人々の状況」について英語で説明してみましょう。

Lack of access to safe drinking water or basic sanitation services	
People's health and quality of life	thousands of children / preventable diseases
	communities / poverty
	women and children / education or other activities

Grammar for Communication

1-27

【すでに終えていることや、経験を伝える表現：現在完了形】

● 現在までに、ある動作が終わっていること（**完了**）、あることを経験したこと（**経験**）、また、過去のある時点からずっとある状態が続いていること（**継続**）を表します。

I have just finished my report. **(完了)**

（たった今、レポートを書き終えました。）

I have been to Boston. **(経験)**

（ボストンに行ったことがあります。）

My uncle has lived in Honolulu for more than ten years. **(継続)**

（私の叔父はホノルルに 10 年以上住んでいます。）

★動画で分かる！
文法解説

Let's Try!

[場面] に合うように、カッコ内の動詞を適切な形に変え , 空所を埋めて英文を完成させましょう。

1. [場面：10 歳の時から、神奈川県の横浜市に住んでいることを伝える。]

   I _____ in Yokohama, Kanagawa Pref. since I was ten years old. (live)

2. [場面：友達とは 10 年来の付き合いであることを伝える。]

   I _____ him for ten years. (know)

3. [場面：彼はアメリカに 3 回行ったことがあることを伝える。]

   He _____ to the U.S.A. three times. (be)

4. [場面：さらにケーキをすすめられて、もうたくさん食べたことを伝える。]

   I _____ enough. Thank you. (have)

5. [場面：いつからサッカークラブに入っているかを聞く。]

   Since when _____ you _____ in the soccer club? (be)

23

Express Yourself

＜自分の経験を述べる＞

自分の経験を、具体例を交えながら説明する練習をします。

Tips:
- 経験を述べる場合は、経験したことを端的に述べ（topic）その内容について具体的な例などを述べ、詳しく説明をしましょう。
- 最後に、自分の意見やコメントなどを述べて話を終わらせましょう。
- 経験したことを述べる際は現在完了形を使いましょう。

  ＊ Lesson 2 で学習した過去の「出来事を説明する」の Tips も参照しましょう。

Let's Try!

Speaking Task:

1. SDGs の各ゴールを達成するための取り組みについて調べ、今まで実践したことがあるもの、あるいはこれから実践したいものについてグループで話し合いましょう。

2. グループで話し合った結果をクラスに英語で報告しましょう。

Writing Task:

SDGs についてどのようなものがあるかを調べ、今まで実践したことがあるもの、あるいはこれから実践したいものについて英語で書いてみましょう。

CAN-DO Check

☑ 私たちの生活における水の大切さと安全な水の確保について理解し、考えることができましたか？ ⑤ ④ ③ ② ①

☑ 自分の経験を伝えることができましたか？ ⑤ ④ ③ ② ①

SDGs

Sustainable Development Goals

Warm-up Questions – Talk in pairs!

1. Do girls and boys need different toys and clothing?

2. Are there different expectations for sons and daughters in your society?

Keywords

Traditional gender stereotypes

Feminine	Masculine
pink	blue
dolls	toy cars
cooking	driving
skirts	pants / trousers
emotional	stoic
passive	active
submissive	aggressive

Conversation

Katie shows Haruki a photograph that she received in a letter from a friend.

Katie: My friend Ella in Sweden just had a baby! Isn't he cute?

Haruki: Yes, he is. What's his name?

Katie: It's Oliver. In Sweden, new parents take time off from work to care for their child. They get a total of 480 days of paid parental leave.

Haruki: That's almost 16 months! I've heard that work-life balance is very important in Sweden.

Katie: That's right. How much time off do new parents get in Japan?

Haruki: I'm not sure. I'll have to look it up!

Useful Expressions

That's almost ....

I've heard that ....

I'm not sure.

Pronunciation

はっきりと聞こえない最後の子音

英語では、語末の子音がはっきりと聞こえないことがあります。例えば child や heard の /d/ がそうです。これは同じ文字でも語頭と語末で発音が異なり、語末では /d/ の口の構えをするものの少し発音を省いているためです。

1. 語末の /d/ の発音を意識して会話練習をしましょう。

2. 同じ d の文字が days の語頭、child と heard の語末でどのように違っているのか話し合いましょう。

27

▶ Reading

1-29
Goal 5 of the SDGs is to "achieve gender equality and empower all women and girls." It states that gender equality is "a necessary foundation for a peaceful, prosperous and sustainable world." Progress has been made over the past few decades. For example, more girls are receiving an education than before. More women are serving in government and leadership positions. Also, laws are being passed to prevent gender discrimination. However, progress is slow, and the global "gender gap" is still a major problem that needs to be solved in many countries. 5

1-30
The gender gap is defined as "a difference between the way men and women are treated in society, or between what men and women do and achieve." The Global Gender Gap Report by the World Economic Forum measures gender equality in four broad categories: Economic Participation and Opportunity, *Educational Attainment, Health and Survival, and *Political Empowerment. We are working on "closing the gap," or reducing global inequality between women and men. 10 15

1-31
The 2021 report states that if current trends continue, we may finally close the overall global gender gap in 135.6 years. If this is true, we will not see a world where men and women are completely equal in our lifetimes, or even our children's lifetimes. However, this number is not set in stone. It may be possible to close the gender gap more quickly. 20

1-32
Globally, the fastest progress is happening in Educational Attainment as well as Health and Survival. This is because of the expansion and accessibility of education for girls in developing countries, as well as improved healthcare conditions. Many developed countries, including Japan, have completely closed the gender gap in primary education; girls 25

and boys receive the same level of education.

1-33

Economic Participation and Opportunity has seen the slowest progress. In many countries, women get paid less than men, and women have to work longer hours to make the same amount of money as men. The 2021 report estimates that the global gender pay gap will take 267.6 years to 30 close.

1-34

Political Empowerment is also progressing slowly. Women are often underrepresented in government positions, and sometimes they are not represented at all. As of January 2021, 81 out of 156 countries had never had a female head of state. The report estimates that *gender parity in 35 politics will take 145.5 years to attain.

1-35

Iceland has been the most gender-equal country for 12 years in a row, followed by Finland, Norway, and New Zealand. The four top-ranking countries all had female prime ministers in 2021. The United Kingdom was ranked 23rd, the United States was ranked 30th, and Japan was ranked 40 120th. Sadly, Japan had the lowest ranking of the G-7 countries. Japan's poor ranking is due to many factors, including women being underrepresented in government and leadership positions, as well as the gender pay gap.

1-36

Fortunately, it doesn't have to stay this way forever. Perhaps in the 45 future, we will see more women become leaders in government and business. No matter your gender, you can help in the global effort to close the gender gap.

Vocabulary

Educational Attainment：教育達成　Political Empowerment：政治関与　gender parity in politics：政治における ジェンダーの平等

Lesson **4**

Gender Equality

Comprehension

Read the passage, and fill in the table below.

本文の内容を参考に The Global Gender Gap Report 2021 の内容を、下表にまとめましょう。

The Global Gender Gap Report 2021 by the World Economic Forum (The World Economic Forum measures gender equality in four broad categories.)	
Economic Participation and Opportunity	It has seen the slowest progress. In many countries, women get paid ( ) than men. Women have to work ( ) hours to make the ( ) amount of money as men.
Educational Attainment	The fastest progress is happening. In primary education of many developed countries, girls and boys receive the ( ) level of education.
Health and Survival	The fastest progress is happening.
Political Empowerment	It is progressing slowly. Women are often underrepresented in ( ) positions, and sometimes they are not represented at all. As of January 2021, 81 out of 156 countries had never had a female ( ) of state.

Answer the Questions

Work with a partner to answer the questions. Use complete sentences.

1. What is Goal 5 of the SDGs?

   ....

2. How can you define "the gender gap?"

   ....

3. According to the 2021 report, how many years do we need to spend to close the overall global gender gap?

   ....

4. What is one of the causes of Japan's poor ranking?

   ....

Discussion Topic

How can you help to solve Goal 5 of the SDGs?

Retelling

次の表とキーワードを参考に、「ジェンダー平等」について英語で説明してみましょう。

THE GLOBAL GENDER GAP INDEX RANKING, 2021

WORLD ECONOMIC FORUM

Global, Top 10

Iceland	(0)		0.892	0.016
Finland	(1)			
Norway	(-1)			
New Zealand	(2)			female prime ministers 2021
Sweden	(-1)		0.823	0.003
Namibia	(6)		0.809	0.025
Rwanda	(2)		0.805	0.014
Lithuania	(25)		0.804	0.059
Ireland	(-2)		0.800	0.002
Switzerland	(8)		0.798	0.019

出典：The Global Gender Gap Report 2021, World Economic Forum

23rd: the United Kingdom
30th: the United States
120th: Japan (= the lowest ranking of the G-7 countries)

gender-equal country　　female prime ministers
the lowest ranking of the G-7 countries　　leadership positions　　the gender pay gap

Grammar for Communication

1-37

【未来のことを伝える表現：未来表現】

◆ 助動詞 will：未来に起こると予想される事柄（～だろう）を表したり、話し手の意志（～します）を表したりします。

We will have a birthday party for my sister tonight. （今夜、妹の誕生会を開きます。）

I will do my best to pass the exam. （試験に合格するために最善を尽くすつもりです。）

◆ 現在進行形 (be＋～ing)：未来を表す修飾語（副詞）とともに使われ、近い未来を表します。

I'm leaving soon. （すぐに出かけます。）

◆ be going to：近い未来に何かが起こると予想されること（～しそうだ）を表したり、前から考えていた予定や意図（～するつもりだ）を表したりします。

I am going to fly to Singapore tomorrow.

（私は明日シンガポールに飛行機で向かいます。）

★動画で分かる！
文法解説

31

[場面] に合うように、カッコ内の動詞を適切な形に変え、空所を埋めて英文を完成させましょう。

1. ［場面：A に来月はどこかに旅行に行くかを聞かれ、京都を訪問する予定だと伝える。］

   A: What's your travel plan next month?

   B: I _____ Kyoto. (visit)

2. ［場面：出かける準備をしていて、A から早く来るように言われ、今行くと伝える。］

   A: Come on! What're you doing?

   B: I _____. (come)

3. ［場面：天気予報によれば、午後は雪が降るということを伝える。］

   The weather forecast reports that it _____ in the afternoon. (snow)

4. ［場面：いつパリに行く予定なのか A に聞かれ、明日出発する予定だと伝える。］

   A: When _____ you _____ to Paris? (go)

   B: I _____ tomorrow. (leave)

5. ［場面：もし明日雨が降れば、明日の試合は中止になることを伝える。］

   If it _____ tomorrow, the game _____ canceled. (rain / be)

Express Yourself

＜自分の意見を述べる＞
自分の意見を論理的に説明する練習を行います。

Tips:
　論理的に意見を説明するためには、次のパターンに沿って考えを述べましょう。
　① 状況：背景となる情報や出来事などを説明する。
　② 問題：どのような問題があるのかを説明する。
　③ 解決：問題に対してどのような解決方法があるかを述べる。
　④ 結果・コメント：解決方法を使うとどのような結果が得られるか、あるいはそれに対する
　　考えなどを述べる。

Exercise:　以下の文章を読み、どの文が上記の①〜④に当たるかを指摘しなさい。

　Many people use smartphones now, but some people use them too much or are addicted to them. These people may suffer from bad eyesight or stiff shoulders. In the worst case, they may fall and injure themselves if they use their phones while walking. One of the best solutions to these problems is to limit the amount of time you spend on your phone. This can reduce tragic accidents and help users to avoid health problems.

Let's Try!

Writing Task:

SDGs の中の Gender Equality について Tips の①状況、②問題、③解決、④結果・コメントの構造に沿って、自分の意見を英語で書きましょう。

Speaking Task:

1. SDGs の中の Gender Equality についてグループで話し合いましょう。

2. グループの意見を Tips の①状況、②問題、③解決、④結果・コメントの構造に沿ってまとめて、クラスに英語で発表しましょう。

CAN-DO Check

☑ 男女共同参画の現状について理解し、ジェンダー平等実現に向　　⑤　④　③　②　①
けた取り組みを考えることができましたか？

☑ 論理的に意見を述べることができましたか？　　　　　　　　　⑤　④　③　②　①

CAN-DO

☑ 着物の変遷について理解することができる。

☑ ある出来事について、事実にもとづいて説明することができる。

Warm-up Questions – Talk in pairs!

1. What style of fashion do you like?

2. What's your favorite item of clothing?

Keywords

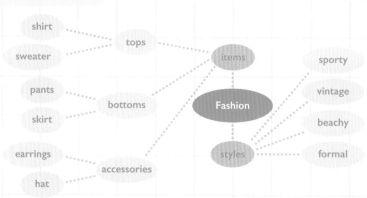

shirt
sweater
tops
items
sporty
pants
bottoms
vintage
skirt
Fashion
beachy
earrings
styles
formal
hat
accessories

▶ Conversation

Haruki's mother sent him some photos from Japan. Haruki shows Katie a photo of a young woman wearing a beautiful kimono.

▶
1-38

Haruki: Look at this picture, Katie. This is my sister, Kyoko.

Katie: Oh! What a beautiful photo!

Haruki: Thank you.

Katie: Why is she wearing a kimono?

Haruki: Many people in Japan wear kimonos for special occasions, like weddings or graduation ceremonies.

Katie: I see!

Haruki: My sister wore a kimono for her coming-of-age ceremony in January. She is twenty years old now.

Useful Expressions

Look at ....

This is ....

What a ...!

Pronunciation

語末の "l"

会話に出てくる "beautiful" と "people" は、単語の末尾に "l" の文字がありますが、日本語の「ル」のような音には聞こえず、「ビューティフォー」、「ピーポー」のように響きます。他にも "l" が終わりにある語をいくつか聞いて耳を鍛えましょう。

Let's Try!

1-39

1. "l" で終わる 6 つの単語の聞き取りをしてみましょう。

1. _____ 2. _____ 3. _____

4. _____ 5. _____ 6. _____

2. 1～6 をもう一度聞き、まねして繰り返してみましょう。

Reading

1-40

The Japanese word "kimono" comes from two words: *kiru*, meaning "to wear," and *mono*, meaning "thing." Its original meaning was "clothing." After *the Meiji Restoration, the word came to signify the traditional Japanese T-shaped robe, as opposed to western-style clothing. Affected by cultural changes, the kimono has gone through many transformations throughout time.

1-41

The first kimonos were influenced by traditional *Han Chinese clothing called *Hanfu*. In the Edo Period, the style of the kimono began to change, reflecting the changing culture. During this time, *the Tokugawa Shogunate ruled Japan as a military government. They imposed a strict class system in which the population was divided into four main classes: samurai, farmers, *artisans, and *merchants. No one was allowed to move up in the hierarchy or change their social status.

1-42

However, the economy was growing quickly, and artisans and merchants became wealthy. They could not use their wealth to move upwards in society, so they focused on creating beautiful textiles, art, and literature. They produced rich kimonos using exquisite fabrics with bold patterns and bright colors.

1-43

With these developments, the Tokugawa Shogunate worried that people would want to rise above their class. They imposed new rules about the fabrics, colors, and techniques used for making kimonos. Soon, new techniques for making kimonos were developed. Subdued colors and subtle patterns were considered elegant and became popular.

1-44

Kimonos changed again with the Meiji Restoration in the late 1860s. Japan had been isolated for a long time, but suddenly, western ideas and

5

10

15

20

25

fashions came flooding into Japan. Influenced by western fashion and art, and free from the rules of the old class system, people began to create dazzling new designs. New techniques for working with silk meant that kimonos were less expensive and more available than ever before.

1-45

Even now, kimonos are popular among Japanese people, although most 30 people have come to wear western-style clothes. Kimonos are still worn for special occasions, such as weddings and graduation ceremonies, or by certain professions, such as sumo wrestlers or geisha. In places like Kyoto, tourists can rent kimonos to wear for souvenir photographs.

1-46

These days, yukatas, lightweight kimonos, are a very popular item in 35 clothing stores not only in Japan, but also in other countries. Colorful yukatas can be seen in Japanese clothing stores abroad, such as UNIQLO, which has many stores in China, France, the U.S., and so on. People often wear yukatas with bright colors and eye-catching patterns to attend summer festivals or fireworks displays. In this way, the kimono has kept 40 the same basic shape for hundreds of years, but its design has always reflected the changes in the culture around it.

Comprehension

Read the passage, and fill in the table below.

時を表す表現に着目して、着物の歴史について、以下の年表にまとめてみましょう。

Time	History of Kimono
Before the Edo Period	*Hanfu* (　　　) clothing influenced Japanese kimonos.
During the Edo Period	Since people were not allowed to change their social status, they spent their (　　　) to produce rich kimonos using exquisite fabrics with bold patterns and bright colors.
	The Tokugawa Shogunate worried and imposed new rules about the kimonos. New (　　　) for making kimonos were developed. Subdued colors and subtle patterns were considered (　　　) and became (　　　).

During the Meiji Restoration in the late 1860s	( ) ideas and fashions came into Japan. People began to create new designs. New techniques for working with silk meant that kimonos were less ( ) and more ( ) than ever before.
The present time	Japanese people wear kimonos for special occasions such as ( ) and ( ) ceremonies. People who have certain ( ) like sumo wrestlers or geisha wear kimonos.
	Yukatas, lightweight kimonos, are very popular ( ). The kimono has kept the same basic shape for hundreds of years, but its design has always reflected the changes in the ( ) around it.

Answer the Questions

Work with a partner to answer the questions. Use complete sentences.

1. What had a great influence on the first Japanese kimonos?

   ....

2. In the Edo Period, what did people focus on because of their unchangeable status?

   ....

3. What happened because of new technologies using silk during the Meiji Restoration?

   ....

4. On what occasions do modern Japanese people wear kimonos?

   ....

5. What do kimono designs reflect?

   ....

Discussion Topic

Do you want to wear a kimono
on special occasions?
Why? / Why not?

Retelling

次のイラストとキーワードを参考に、「日本人が着物をどんな時に着るか、どんな職業の人が着るか」について英語で説明してみましょう。

Japanese people	(for) special occasions	(by) certain professions
kimonos	weddings / graduation ceremonies	sumo wrestlers / geisha

Grammar for Communication

1-47

【可能性や推量を述べる表現：助動詞① can, may】

◆ can / could：〜できる / できた（能力）、〜かもしれない（可能性）、〜することができる / 〜してもよい（許可）

The Shinkansen can travel between Tokyo and Shin-Osaka in about two-and-a-half hours.

（新幹線は東京―新大阪間を約2時間半で走行できます。）（可能）

You can use my computer.

（私のコンピューターを使ってもいいですよ。）（許可）

＊可能性の意味の否定 cannot は「〜のはずがない」という意味になることに注意しましょう。

＊許可の意味の場合、could のほうが can より丁寧な表現になります。

◆ may / might：〜してもよい（許可）、〜かもしれない（推量）

May I use your computer?

（あなたのコンピューターを使わせていただけますか。）（許可）

My mother might be here soon.

（母はすぐに到着するかもしれない。）（推量）

★動画で分かる！
文法解説

［場面］に合うように、助動詞を使って（　）の部分を書き直しましょう。または、英文全体を疑問文にしましょう。

1. ［場面：Ken が会議に時間どおりに到着しないかもしれないという気持ちを表す。］

   Ken (arrives) in time for the meeting.

2. ［場面：テストで満点を取ったと聞いて、そんなはずはないという気持ちを伝える。］

   A: I got a perfect score.

   B: That (isn't) true. You didn't study.

3. ［場面：お願いしたいという依頼の気持ちを丁寧に伝える。］

   (You do me a favor.)

4. ［場面：Lucy の email address を知っているか聞かれ、David が知っているかもしれないという気持ちを伝える。］

   A: Do you know Lucy's email address?

   B: David (knows) it.

5. ［場面：同窓会で知った顔の人にあったがすぐに名前が思い出せなかったことを伝える。］

   I saw a man at the reunion party, but I (remember) his name immediately.

Express Yourself

＜報告（レポート）をする＞
ある事柄の出来事や歴史について、事実に基づいて説明し、そのことに対しての自分の考察やコメントを述べる練習をします。

Tips:

ここでは Lesson 4 で学んだ次の 2 つのパターンを使用して、報告（レポート）をします。
①状況（背景となる情報や出来事の説明）
②結果・コメント（どのような結果となったか、またそれに対する自分の意見を簡単に述べる。）
＊状況について書く場合は、Lesson 2 で学んだ「過去の出来事について説明する」も参照しましょう。

Speaking Task:

グループになり、下のトピックの中から一つ選んで、その歴史をウェブサイトで調べて、結果を
クラスに英語で発表しましょう。

Topics:
- jeans
- wigs
- skirts
- others

Writing Task:

上のトピックの中から一つ選んで、自分で調べた情報を英語でまとめて報告しましょう。

CAN-DO Check

☑ 着物の変遷について理解することができましたか？　　　　　⑤　④　③　②　①

☑ ある出来事について、事実にもとづいて説明することができま　⑤　④　③　②　①
　したか？

Lesson

5

Fashion

CAN-DO

☑ 食と文化の関係について理解することができる。

☑ 相手にアドバイスをすることができる。

Warm-up Questions – Talk in pairs!

1. What kinds of food do you like to eat?

2. What's your favorite ethnic food?

► Keywords

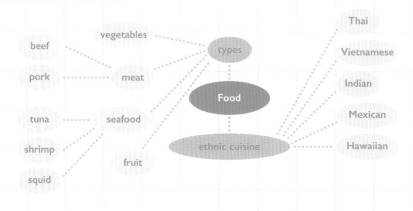

Conversation

Katie is looking at the website for a sushi restaurant.

1-48

Katie: Haruki, I'm writing an article about a sushi restaurant for the school newspaper. I'm going there tonight. Will you come and help me?

Haruki: Sure! What's the name of the restaurant?

Katie: It's called Donny's Sushi. It's famous for its original sushi rolls.

Haruki: That sounds great! I love sushi rolls.

Katie: Perfect! So, you'll help me with the article?

Haruki: Well, I can help you with tasting the sushi.

Useful Expressions

Will you ...?

That sounds great!

Perfect!

Pronunciation

イントネーション 2

会話に出てくる "Sure!" と "Perfect!" の抑揚を注意して聞くと、高い声から低い声へ思い切り下がっていることがわかります。このように声の高さを大きく変化させることで、話し手は、話題に対する「興味」「熱意」や「興奮」を伝えます。反対に、声を下げてから上げると「質問」に聞こえます。また、声の高低の変化が乏しい話し方は、「無関心」と思われやすいことが様々な研究からわかっています。

Let's Try!

1-49

1. 1〜4のイントネーションを意識して聞いて、まねして繰り返してみましょう。
   1. All right.（通常） 2. All right!（興味） 3. All right?（質問）
   4. All right...（無関心）

1-50

2. 下記の（ ）に抑揚を曲線で描き、ペアで話し合いましょう。解答例を参考にしましょう。
   解答例：All right?（↪）
   1. All right!（ ） 2. All right.（ ） 3. All right?（ ）
   4. Singapore!（ ） 5. Singapore?（ ） 6. Yes...（ ） 7. Yes!（ ）

Reading

Donny's Sushi

★★★★★ Critics' choice

Donny's Sushi brings a taste of Japan to New England
by Katie McLaughlin

1-51
    Donny's Sushi in downtown Boston opened its doors at the end of last month, and it has enjoyed immense popularity with both locals and tourists. Its menu has a wide selection of both traditional Japanese dishes as well as more creative, modern dishes. The menu also features original items created by the manager and main chef, Donald "Donny" Ozawa.   5

1-52
    Mr. Ozawa was born in Los Angeles, California, and he moved to Boston ten years ago. His parents, who are from Japan, taught him about Japanese cooking from a young age. After graduating from high school, he went to *culinary school in San Francisco, where his teacher inspired him to begin creating his own recipes. After he finished school, he started work as a   10 chef at a restaurant in San Francisco's *Japantown.

1-53
    At the restaurant, he created a special sushi roll that he called the "Donny Roll." It contains shrimp tempura and spicy mayonnaise on the inside, with black sesame seeds on the outside. After the Donny Roll exploded in popularity, he decided that he wanted to open his own   15 restaurant. His chance came when an acquaintance told him about an opportunity to manage a new restaurant in Boston.

1-54
    "Sushi has been enjoyed in Japan for centuries," said Mr. Ozawa. "Recently, it has also gained popularity in the United States, where it is praised as a health food. Sushi rolls called *makizushi* are very popular, and   20 this allows me to experiment with different fillings. I have a special place in my heart for traditional Japanese sushi, but I also enjoy combining ingredients in original ways."

1-55
    The menu at Donny's Sushi includes many types of raw fish, such as

tuna, salmon, and mackerel. Vegetable rolls are available for vegetarians 25 and people who cannot eat raw seafood. Of course, don't forget American favorites such as the California Roll, Alaskan Roll, and Philadelphia Roll (made with real Philadelphia cream cheese).

1-56

There is also a special section of original sushi rolls created by Mr. Ozawa. The Donny Roll is one of his most popular items. Customers also 30 love the Lobster Roll, which contains cooked lobster meat and mayonnaise. Mr. Ozawa says that this was inspired by the popular New England sandwich, the lobster roll, which is a hot dog bun filled with lobster meat and mayonnaise. "I was born on the West Coast, where the California Roll originated," says Mr. Ozawa. "Now that I live on the East Coast, I can 35 experience a different point of view. I'm always looking for new and interesting ideas."

1-57

Indeed, customers can always experience something new and interesting at Donny's Sushi. The restaurant is open daily for lunch from 11:30 a.m. to 3 p.m., and for dinner from 5 p.m. to 10 p.m. Please call 40 during business hours for reservations.

Vocabulary

culinary school：調理学校　**Japantown**：日本街（19 世紀から 20 世紀前半にかけて大量の日本人が、アメリカ西海岸へ移住して発展した町）

Comprehension

Read the passage, and fill in the table below.

Donald "Donny" Ozawa の情報を英語でまとめてみましょう。

Information	Donald "Donny" Ozawa
Birthplace	He was born in (　　　　), California.
After graduating from high school	He went to (　　　) school in San Francisco.
How Mr. Ozawa's teacher inspired him	He was inspired to (　　　　) his own (　　　).
After graduating from culinary school	He started work as a (　　　　) in San Francisco's (　　　).

What he created at a restaurant in Japantown	He created a special sushi roll called the "( ) ( )."
What Mr. Ozawa heard from an acquaintance	Mr. Ozawa's acquaintance told him about an opportunity to ( ) a new restaurant in ( ).
The menu at Donny's Sushi	Donny Roll ( ) ( ) such as the California Roll, Alaskan Roll, and Philadelphia Roll Lobster Roll
The restaurant is open	daily for ( ) from 11:30 a.m. to 3 p.m. daily for ( ) from 5 p.m. to 10 p.m.

Answer the Questions

Work with a partner to answer the questions. Use complete sentences.

1. With whom has Donny's Sushi enjoyed immense popularity?

   ....

2. Who inspired Mr. Ozawa to create his own recipes?

   ....

3. When did Mr. Ozawa decide to open his own restaurant?

   ....

4. Why is sushi praised in the United States recently?

   ....

5. What do customers who visit Donny's Sushi expect?

   ....

Discussion Topic

What kind of food would
you recommend to tourists
from foreign countries?

46

Retelling

アメリカ・カリフォルニア州ロサンジェルス生まれの Mr. Ozawa が生み出した "Donny Roll" について、次のイラストとキーワードを参考に、英語で説明してみましょう。

Donny Roll		
Mr. Ozawa　a new style special sushi roll	inside	
	shrimp tempura / spicy mayonnaise	
	outside	
"Donny Roll"	black sesame seeds	

学・創

Grammar for Communication

1-58

【相手に助言をしたり、しなければならないことを伝えたりする表現：助動詞②：should, must】

◆ **should**：〜したほうがよい **(提案)**、〜するべきだ **(義務)** 〜当然だ **(当然)**

You should take this medicine. （この薬を飲んだ方がいいです。） **(提案)**
You should pay the bill here. （お勘定はここで払う必要があります。） **(義務)**
It is natural that she should think so. （彼女がそう考えるのは当然です。） **(当然)**

＊ should have＋過去分詞　は（〜するべきだったのに）という意味を表します。

◆ **must**：〜しなければならない **(義務)**、〜にちがいない **(推定)**

You must attend the next meeting.
（あなたは次の会議に出席しなければなりません。） **(義務)**
The man must be a teacher. （あの男性は教師に違いありません。） **(推定)**

＊ must have＋過去分詞　は（〜だったに違いない）という意味を表します。

場面に合うように、助動詞を使って（　）の部分を書き直しましょう。

1. ［場面：相手に黙っているべきだったという気持ちを伝える。］

You (keep) your mouth shut.

47

2. ［場面：パーティに呼ぶべきだったのにという気持ちを伝える。］

You (invite) Chris to the party.

3. ［場面：宝くじがあたったと聞いて、からかっているのだろうという気持ちを伝える。］

A: I won the lottery!

B: You (be) kidding!

4. ［場面：我々のアドバイスを聞くべきだという気持ちを伝える。］

You (follow) our advice.

5. ［場面：閉店する前にスーパーに行かなければならないという気持ちを伝える。］

I (go) to the supermarket before it closes.

Express Yourself

＜アドバイスをする＞

相手にアドバイスをする練習をします。アドバイスする際には次のような表現を使います。

Tips:
- advise, recommend などの動詞を使う。
- 助動詞 should, had better, must を使う。

Exercise:

下の単語から空所に入るものを選び、適切な形に変え，空所を埋めて英文を完成させましょう。

1. I .... that you visit the Louvre Museum.

2. Catherine .... me to take some medicine before going to bed.

3. You .... wear appropriate clothes when you go to an interview.

4. You .... exceed the speed limit when you drive a car.

5. You .... slurp your noodles in Japan.

must   advise   can   recommend   should

Speaking Task:

グループで、外国から日本に来る観光客に対しての「日本における食事のマナー」ついてアドバイスするべきことを話し合い、クラスに英語で報告しましょう。

Writing Task:

Speaking Task で話し合った内容を英語でまとめましょう。

(Extra work)

下のトピックの中から一つ選び、外国から日本に来る観光客へのアドバイスを英語で書きましょう。

Topics:「食事の仕方」「温泉の入り方」「電車の乗り方」

CAN-DO Check

☑ 食と文化の関係について理解することができましたか？ ⑤ ④ ③ ② ①

☑ 相手にアドバイスをすることができましたか？ ⑤ ④ ③ ② ①

49

The History of YouTube

Warm-up Questions – Talk in pairs!

1. What types of videos do you like to watch on YouTube?

2. Do you follow any channels on YouTube?

▶ Keywords

Types of YouTube videos

cooking

beauty

fashion

gaming   music

meditation & relaxation

movies & TV   sports & fitness

travel

funny animals

educational

product reviews

business

Conversation

Haruki looks very tired. Katie asks him if something is wrong.

1-59

Haruki: I'm so sleepy. I didn't sleep very well last night.

Katie: Hmm. What were you doing just before going to bed?

Haruki: Let's see... I was lying in bed and watching YouTube videos on my smartphone.

Katie: That's it! The light from your screen can mess up your body's sleep cycle.

Haruki: Actually, my smartphone helps me sleep.

Katie: How does it do that?

Haruki: I found a YouTube video that plays the soothing sound of ocean waves.

Useful Expressions

Let's see...

That's it!

Actually

Pronunciation

YouTube の発音

皆さんは YouTube をどう発音していますか？実は英語話者の間では 3 種類の発音があります。tube の出だしを① two、② chew、③「テュー」のように発音する人がいるようです。

Let's Try!

1. アメリカに留学している春樹は上の①〜③のどの発音をしていましたか？

1-59

2. a〜c は、①〜③のどの発音か聞いて確認しましょう。

   a（   ）b（   ）c（   ）

1-60

Reading

Many people today, especially young people, report that they spend more time watching YouTube than watching traditional TV. They enjoy being able to watch whatever they want whenever they want, without the limitations of a TV station's rules or schedule. YouTubers sometimes seem more honest and relatable than traditional movie actors or TV reporters. You can find information and/or entertainment related to almost any topic, and there is a sense of belonging and community among fans or people with common interests.

When children are asked what they want to be in the future, "a YouTuber" has become a popular answer. Uploading videos seems like a fun and creative way to become famous and make money. However, people are becoming aware of the mental, emotional, and sometimes physical *toll that many YouTubers face. It is stressful to put your private life in the public eye for anyone in the world to *anonymously comment on. YouTube has grown *exponentially and changed dramatically since it was created. Its founders probably couldn't have imagined its current form.

YouTube started with a simple idea. Its founders, Steve Chen, Chad Hurley, and Jawed Karim, met when they were working at the company Paypal in Silicon Valley. They were frustrated because it wasn't easy to share videos over the Internet in 2005. They decided to make a website to upload, share, and view content freely.

They registered the site in February 2005 and uploaded the first video in April of that year. The video was a short clip of Karim at the San Diego Zoo, appropriately titled "Me at the Zoo." People loved the idea of sharing their own videos, and the site quickly became popular, although this early version looked very different from today. For example, there were no *ads, there was a ten-minute limit on video clips, and the "like," "comment," and "subscribe" features did not exist.

1-65

In 2005, Google was working to create a similar service called Google Video, but it was not as popular. Susan Wojcicki, a marketing manager at Google, noticed that YouTube was successfully competing against much larger, more powerful companies. She proposed that Google buy the small company. In November 2006, Google purchased YouTube for $1.65 billion. Many companies wanted to display ads on the popular site. Starting in 2007, YouTube focused on creating an advertising system to *monetize the site's content.

1-66

In February 2014, Susan Wojcicki became the CEO of YouTube. In the mostly male-dominated world of technology companies, she is an advocate for causes such as expanding *paid family leave, fighting gender discrimination, and supporting women and girls who are interested in computer science. Many of her ideas and innovations shaped YouTube into its current form.

1-67

YouTube will probably continue to change and evolve in the future. Do you want to be a YouTuber yourself someday, or do you just want to enjoy watching interesting videos? If you had a chance to upload a video on YouTube, what kind of clip would you want to show your audience of people from around the world?

Vocabulary
(health) toll：健康被害　anonymously comment：匿名のコメントをする　exponentially：急激に
ads（＝advertisements）：広告　monetize：収益化する　paid family leave：有給の育児休暇

Comprehension

Read the passage, and fill in the table below.
時間の表現に着目して、YouTube の変遷を英語でまとめてみましょう。

TIME	DESCRIPTIONS
2005	YouTube founders, Steve Chen, Chad Hurley, and Jawed Karim, decided to make a website to upload and share videos over the Internet (　　　) and view content (　　　).

February 2005	They ( ) the website.
April 2005	They uploaded the first ( ). The early version of YouTube had no ( ), a ten-minute limit on video clips, and the "like," "comment," and "subscribe" ( ) did not exist.
November 2006	( ) purchased YouTube for $1.65 billion. Many companies wanted to display ( ) on YouTube.
2007	YouTube focused on creating an advertising system to monetize the site's content.
February 2014	Susan Wojcicki became the CEO of YouTube.

Answer the Questions

Work with a partner to answer the questions. Use complete sentences.

1. What problems do many YouTubers face?

....

2. Why were the founders of YouTube frustrated in 2005?

....

3. What was the title of the first video uploaded to YouTube in April 2005?

....

4. What kinds of causes does Susan Wojcicki advocate for?

....

Discussion Topic

Do you think YouTube will continue to change and evolve in the future?

Retelling

内のキーワードを参考に、「YouTube のはじまり」について ___ に続けて英語で説明してみましょう。

> uploaded / the first video
> the early version / no ads / a ten-minute limit on video clips
> the "like," "comment," and "subscribe" features / not exist

> YouTube founders, Steve Chen, Chad Hurley, and Jawed Karim registered the site in February 2005 and uploaded the first video in April of that year.

Grammar for Communication

【比較をする表現①】

1-68

◆ 比較級：〈形容詞 / 副詞 er〉もしくは〈more / less 形容詞 / 副詞〉than 〜

（あるものと比較して程度が高い / 低いことを表します。）

The summer in England is cooler than that of Japan.

（イングランドの夏は日本の夏と比べて涼しい。）

◆ 最上級：the ＋形容詞＋ est / the ＋ most / least 形容詞 / 副詞（形容詞 / 副詞＋ est）

（あるものと比較して最も程度が高い / 低いことを表します。）

The budget for this year is the largest in 10 years.

（今年の予算は、10 年間で最も大きい。）

★動画で分かる！
文法解説

Let's Try!

[ ] 内の伝えたい内容に合わせて、比較表現を用いて英文を書き変えましょう。

1. Tim is 20 years old, and Kent is 22 years old.
   [Kent が Tim よりも 2 歳年上だということを伝える。]

   [   ]

2. The birth rate in Japan was about 2 in the 1970s, but it is about 1.4 now.
   [出生率が 1970 年代に比べて、今の方が低くなっていることを伝える。]

   [   ]

3. The population of Tokyo is about 1.3 million. There are no other prefectures that have such a huge population.
   [東京の人口が日本で一番多いことを伝える。]

   [   ]

55

The History of YouTube

Lesson
7

4. Moira got a perfect exam score, and nobody else in the class got such a high score.

   [Moira がクラスの中で、試験で最も高い点を取ったことを伝える。]

   [   ]

5. I had expected to get a score of 100 on the exam. In fact, I got a score of 95.

   [思っていたよりも試験の点数が悪かったと伝える。]

   [   ]

Express Yourself

＜利点・欠点について述べる＞

利点・欠点について自分の意見を述べる練習を行います。

Tips:

利点・欠点について自分の意見を述べる場合は、次のような手順で考えます。

1. あるトピックに関してどのような利点・欠点がいくつあるかを考える。
2. 意見を述べる場合は、あるトピックについて、いくつの欠点があるかをはじめに述べる。(それぞれの利点・欠点について簡潔に説明を入れるとよい。)
3. それぞれの利点・欠点について具体例を交えて説明をする。
4. 最後に、もう一度どのような利点・欠点があったかをまとめる。

Exercise:

スマートフォンの利点 / 欠点について書かれた次の文章を完成させましょう。

Many people use smartphones now. I think there are three (1) .... points for

using them: (2) ...., (3) .... and (4) ....

First, (5) ....

Secondly, (6) ....

And finally, (7) ....

For these reasons, I think smartphones are (8) .... for us.

Let's Try!

Speaking Task:

1. 下のトピックの中から一つ選び、利点と欠点についてグループで英語で話し合いましょう。

Topics:
● Social media

- YouTube
- Internet
- Wikipedia
- Google Translate
- Others

2. 話し合いの結果をまとめて、クラスに英語で報告しましょう。

Writing Task:

上のトピックの中から一つ選び、利点と欠点をまとめ、英語で書いてみましょう。

CAN-DO Check

☑ YouTube の歴史と発展した理由を理解することができましたか？　　⑤　④　③　②　①

☑ ものごとの利点と欠点について述べることができましたか？　　⑤　④　③　②　①

Warm-up Questions – Talk in pairs!

1. Where would you like to go on a study abroad program?

2. What are your goals for studying abroad?

▶ Keywords

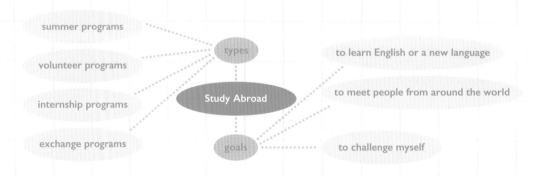

summer programs

volunteer programs

internship programs

exchange programs

types

Study Abroad

goals

to learn English or a new language

to meet people from around the world

to challenge myself

Conversation

Professor Wong is a Chinese-language professor and the head of the Asian Studies Department at Haruki's college. She asks him a question.

2-01

Professor Wong: Haruki, may I speak to you for a moment?

Haruki: Of course, Professor Wong. What is it?

Professor Wong: The Asian Studies Department is making a new website. We want to encourage more students to study abroad.

Haruki: I see.

Professor Wong: Could you write an article about why you decided to study abroad in the U.S.?

Haruki: An article?

Professor Wong: Yes. I think that it would be interesting to students who are thinking of studying in another country.

Useful Expressions

May I ...?

Of course.

Could you ...?

Pronunciation

カタカナ英語に注意しよう

もともとは英語で、日本語でも使われるようになった語を外来語と呼びます。「ミルク」のようにカタカナで外来語を書くと、一目で漢字やひらがなと区別でき、大変便利です。但し、カタカナ表記の英語は、本来の発音と全く異なる場合が多く、聞く時も話す時も注意が必要です。例えば、会話では Asian と website に気をつけましょう。Asian は、アジアンではなく「エィジャ n」のように聞こえます。website は「ウェ b サイ t」のように響き、「ウェ」と「サイ」はハッキリ聞こえますが、「ブ」と「ト」は聞こえ難くなります。

Let's Try!

2-02

1. 英単語を書き取りましょう。外来語として定着しているものばかりです。

    1. _____   2. _____   3. _____

    4. _____   5. _____

2. お手本の音声を聞き、各語の最も際立った箇所に印をつけ、まねして発音してみましょう。

Reading

I'm Haruki Yamamoto, an exchange student from Kanagawa, Japan. I left my home and my college in Japan to study at a college in Boston, Massachusetts for one year. I am enjoying my time in the U.S., and I have made friends from many countries, who have many different points of view. I would recommend studying abroad to anyone who is considering it. 5

When I was in elementary school, I wanted to be a baseball player. I used to watch baseball on TV with my father. We followed our favorite teams and players. One day, my favorite player announced that he was joining a team in the United States. When he played abroad, I noticed the faces of kids like me in the crowd. I found myself wishing that I could talk 10 to them and become friends. However, despite my interest, I didn't know how to go about studying English.

Like most Japanese students, I started studying English in junior high school. My teacher in elementary school had inspired me to become interested in science. At that time, I was more interested in science class 15 than English class. My mind was full of interesting inventions and experiments. I dreamed of *rocket ships and *far-off planets. I was going to be a scientist! I didn't see the need to learn English.

In high school, my mother suggested that I listen to an English language program on the radio. For fun, I listened to it every day while eating 20 breakfast before school. The hosts of the show seemed to be enjoying themselves as they talked and joked. Slowly, I was able to pick out words and phrases that I could understand. Soon, I found myself laughing along with them.

Then, one day, they interviewed a scientist on the radio show. He talked 25

about how learning English had allowed him to work with engineers for *NASA in the United States. I felt as if a bolt of lightning had hit me. English wasn't just for fun anymore. English could help me achieve my dreams! From then on, I worked hard in both science class and English class.

2-08

After I passed my exams and graduated from high school, I continued 30 to study English at college in Japan. I decided to study abroad in my junior year. I chose this college in Boston, and here I am! I am still working towards achieving my dreams. I believe that experiencing another culture and learning another language broadens your horizons. I think it is important whether you are interested in baseball, science, history, 35 literature, or dance. You can chase your dream in cities like Boston, London, Paris, Vancouver, Beijing, or Tokyo. I urge you to take a chance!

Vocabulary
rocket ship(s)：宇宙船　**far-off planet(s)**：はるか彼方の惑星
NASA（＝National Aeronautics and Space Administration）：アメリカ航空宇宙局

Comprehension

Read the passage, and fill in the table below.
「春樹が留学するまでの過程」を以下の表にまとめてみましょう。

春樹が留学するまでの過程		
出身地		日本　神奈川県
小学校時代	将来の夢	
	よくしていたこと	父親とテレビで（　　　）すること
	お気に入りの野球選手がきっかけで興味を持ったこと	海外の子供と（　　　）になること
	問題点	（　　　　　）がわからなかった
中学校時代	先生の影響で興味を持ったもの	（　　　）に興味を持ち、（　　　）と（　　　）で頭がいっぱいだった
	将来の夢	科学者になり、惑星に（　　　）を打ち上げること
高校時代	母親が薦めた英語の学習方法	（　　　）で英語の番組を聞くこと
	科学者のインタビューをラジオで聞いて気づいたこと	
大学時代	決心したこと	大学３年次にボストンの大学に（　　　）することと

Answer the Questions

Work with a partner to answer the questions. Use complete sentences.

1. What was Haruki's wish when he saw the faces of kids on TV when he was in elementary school?

   ....

2. In junior high school, which subject was Haruki interested in?

   ....

3. What did Haruki's mother suggest for him to do?

   ....

4. What made Haruki feel as if a bolt of lightning had hit him?

   ....

5. What does Haruki believe is important for achieving one's dreams?

   ....

Discussion Topic

What do you think you can
learn through studying
abroad?

Retelling

「ラジオ番組のインタビューコーナーで、ある科学者が英語学習について話しているのを聴いた春樹が感じたこと」について、次のイラストとキーワードを参考に、英語で説明してみましょう。

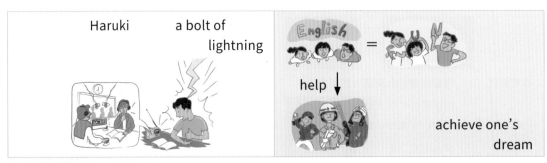

Haruki felt ....

【比較をする表現②】

2-09　比較に関する表現を確認します。

◆ not so much ~ as …　（~というよりもむしろ…）

He is not so much a scholar as a politician.　（彼は学者というよりもむしろ政治家です。）

◆ the 比較級~, the 比較級…　（~すればするほど、ますます…）

The higher you go up, the lower the temperature becomes.

（高く上がれば上がるほど、ますます温度が下がります。）

◆ more and more　（ますます多くの~）

More and more people from other countries visit Japan.

（ますます多くの海外からの人々が日本を訪れています。）

◆ as+形容詞/副詞+possible, as+形容詞/副詞+as 主語+can (could)…　（できるだけ~）

Please finish this task as soon as possible.

（この仕事をできるだけ早く終わらせてください。）

★動画で分かる！
文法解説

◆ ~ times as 形容詞/副詞 as…　（…の~倍）

This dog is three times as big as that one.

（この犬はあの犬の3倍の大きさです。）

Lesson
8

Study Abroad

Let's Try!

［　］の伝えたい内容に合わせて、比較表現を用いて英文を書き変えましょう。

1. The price of the large bowl is 1,000 yen. The price of the small bowl is 4,000 yen.

　［the small bowl は the large bowl の4倍の値段がすることを伝える。］

　［　　　　　　　　　　　　　　　　　　　　　　　　　　　　　　　　　　　　　　　］

2. If the weather is cooler, I feel better.

　［「the 比較, the 比較」の表現を使って同様の意味を伝える。］

　［　　　　　　　　　　　　　　　　　　　　　　　　　　　　　　　　　　　　　　　］

3. He is a scholar rather than a teacher.

　［not so much ~ as…を使って同じ内容を伝える。］

　［　　　　　　　　　　　　　　　　　　　　　　　　　　　　　　　　　　　　　　　］

4. Last year, we had many hot days over 34 degrees Celsius, but this year, we had even more.

　［「more and more」の表現を使って、ますます34℃を超える暑い日が増えていることを伝える。］

　［　　　　　　　　　　　　　　　　　　　　　　　　　　　　　　　　　　　　　　　］

5. The new tablet costs 50,000 yen, but the second-hand one, 25,000 yen.
   [中古のタブレットの値段は新品のものの半分であることを伝える。]

   [   ]

Express Yourself

＜列挙して説明をする＞

重要な事柄を伝えるときには、箇条書きにする方が効果的な場合があります。ここでは、箇条書きに列挙して説明する仕方を練習します。

Tips:

- 箇条書きにするときのポイントには次のようなものがあります。
- 名詞句、動詞句、動名詞句、不定詞句、簡潔な文で要点を表しましょう。
- 箇条書きにした内容の前に番号や丸を付けましょう。
- 口頭で説明する場合は、箇条書きの文が完全な文でない場合は、完全な文で説明しましょう。
- 箇条書きにした内容の詳しい事柄を口頭で説明しましょう。

Exercise:

次の下線の英文を箇条書きにしてみましょう。

Here are some important business rules in Japan:
(1) You should be punctual.
(2) You should wear a suit.
(3) You should have your business cards with you all the time.
These rules are very important for your success in Japanese business settings.

(1) ....
(2) ....
(3) ....

Speaking Task:

1. グループで、「留学で必要だと思われること / もの」について英語で話し合いましょう。

2. 話し合った結果を、スライドに箇条書きにしてクラスに英語で発表しましょう。

Writing Task:

「留学で必要だと思われること / もの」について、発表に基づいて自分の意見を英語で書きましょう。

CAN-DO Check

☑ 海外留学の意義について理解することができましたか？ ⑤ ④ ③ ② ①

☑ 重要な事柄について列挙して説明することができましたか？ ⑤ ④ ③ ② ①

College Life in the U.S.

CAN-DO

☑ 日本とアメリカの大学生活の違いについて理解することができる。

☑ ものごとを比較・対照して説明することができる。

Warm-up Questions – Talk in pairs!

1. What is your favorite class or subject? Why?

2. What do you do on campus when you're not studying?

Keywords

on-campus

off-campus

part-time jobs

internships

job hunting

jobs

clubs

activities

College Life

classes

assignments

presentations

exams

grades

volunteer work

academics

seminars

projects

research

Conversation

Haruki sees Katie sitting at a desk in the library surrounded by piles of papers and books. Her face looks tired, and she is writing in a notebook.

2-10

Haruki: Hi, Katie. You look a little stressed. Is everything all right?

Katie: I'm OK. I just have a lot of work to do. I have to give three presentations on Thursday!

Haruki: Three presentations in one day?

Katie: Yes. I hope I can finish in time.

Haruki: Good luck!

Katie: Thanks. After all of my presentations are finished, TGIF!

Haruki: TGIF?

Katie: Thank goodness, it's Friday! Then, I can relax on the weekend!

Useful Expressions

You look ....
Is everything all right?
Good luck!

Pronunciation

略語の発音

略語の発音には、主に2通りあります。①1文字ずつ読むもの（例：TGIF）と、②1つの語のように読むもの（例：UNESCO）です。また、ASAP（as soon as possible）のように、どちらの読み方も聞かれるものもあります。

Let's Try!

2-11

1. 略語を聞いて、書いてみましょう。

　　1. _____ 2. _____ 3. _____

　　4. _____ 5. _____ 6. _____

2. お手本の音声を聞き、発音してみましょう。

Reading

To: Kyoko
From: Haruki
Subject: Hi

Hi Kyoko,

How are you? How are Mom and Dad? The other day, Mom sent me a letter and a picture of you holding our cat Maru. I miss you all! I am writing to you on the lawn in front of my dormitory. We have nice weather today, so most of the students are outside. 5

College life in the States is very different from college life in Japan. Now I know the meaning of the phrase "culture shock." In my classes in Japan, I always sat quietly and listened to the professor's lectures. Sometimes the professor called on students to see if they were paying attention, but students almost never interrupted the professor's lecture with their own 10 opinions on the material. I expected my college experience in the United States to be different, but I was surprised by some of the differences.

As I walked onto the campus, I was surprised by the groups of students sitting on the lawn. They take their books and notebooks outside, and they study together with friends. Sometimes, if the weather is nice, professors 15 go outside to teach! Sitting on the grass with my classmates listening to my professor is quite different from sitting in a quiet classroom. I wondered if we could actually learn anything with the bright sun and the cool breeze as *distractions. However, now I find that I feel refreshed and energized during an outdoor class. 20

Classes are different, too. I have to participate in group discussions or give a presentation in class almost every day. Students are expected to raise their hands and ask questions, even in the middle of a professor's lecture. Sometimes, I have to give my opinion even when I am not sure of myself. I

remember the first time my professor suddenly asked, "What do you think, 25
Haruki?" and I froze. Everyone was looking at me, so I had to force myself
to speak up! All of the other students seem eager to give their opinions, so I
have tried to make my voice heard as well. Slowly but surely, these
experiences changed me. I have become more confident when speaking in
front of others. 30

2-16

On the weekends here, there are lots of events and parties.
Participating in events is a great way to relax and forget about the stress of
homework and tests. The other day, I went to an Indian festival called
Diwali. It was hosted by the Asian Studies department. We ate delicious
Indian food prepared by students, and many people wore traditional Indian 35
clothing. Next weekend, I will go to a poetry reading by the Creative
Writing department and also a football game. I can't wait!

I hope things are great at home! Talk to you later!

Haruki

Vocabulary
distraction(s)：気を散らすもの（ここでは勉強の邪魔になるようなもの）

Comprehension

Read the passage, and fill in the table below.

本文の内容を参考に、アメリカのキャンパスライフと日本のキャンパスライフを以下の表を使って比較してみましょう。

College life in the U.S.		
	Japan	**U.S.**
学生の様子	学生たちは、教室で、教授の講義を（　　　　）に聴いている。	学生たちは（　　　　）に本やノートを持ち出して、友人と学習する。天気がよければ、（　　　　）に座って、講義を受けることもある。
教室の様子	教授たちは、学生たちが授業に集中しているか確認する。授業中、自分たちの（　　　　）を述べて、教授の講義を中断させることはほとんどない。	ほぼ毎回、グループで話し合いをしたり、（　　　　）をしたりしている。講義中でも、手を挙げて（　　　　）する。学生たちは、積極的に自分の（　　　　）を述べる。
週末の過ごし方		イベントやパーティに参加することで、宿題やテストのストレス発散をしている。

Answer the Questions

Work with a partner to answer the questions. Use complete sentences.

1. What is the phrase Haruki has understood through college life in the U.S.?

   ....

2. What do Japanese students usually do during their lectures?

   ....

3. How does Haruki feel about outdoor classes now?

   ....

4. What are the students in the U.S. eager to do during their lectures?

   ....

5. How do the students in the U.S. spend their weekends?

   ....

Discussion Topic

How do you want to study
in your classes at college?

Retelling

「アメリカの大学生が授業中に求められること」について、次のイラストとキーワードを参考に、英語で説明してみましょう。

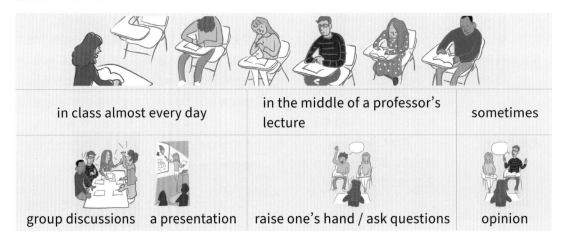

in class almost every day	in the middle of a professor's lecture	sometimes
group discussions a presentation	raise one's hand / ask questions	opinion

Classes in the States are different from those in Japan. Students

even when I am not sure of myself.

Grammar for Communication

2-17

【視点を変えて説明したり、〜させると伝えたりする表現：受け身、使役】

◆ 受け身：「be 動詞＋過去分詞」（〜される）

Our house was built by my father.

（私たちの家は父によって建てられました。→　父が建てました。）

＊完了形とともに受け身が使われる場合は［have＋been＋過去分詞］、進行形とともに使われる場合は［be＋being＋過去分詞］の形になります。

◆ 使役：make, get, have は、[make ＋人 / もの＋動詞の原形] の文型のとき「〜させる / される」という意味を表します。

The teacher made his students study hard.　（先生は学生たちを熱心に勉強させました。）

[get＋人 / もの＋to do/ 現在分詞 / 過去分詞]

I got my car repaired.　（私は車を修理してもらいました。）

[have＋人 / もの＋動詞の原形 / 現在分詞 / 過去分詞]

I had my hair cut.　（私は髪を切ってもらいました。）

★動画で分かる！
文法解説

Let's Try!

[　　] の指示に従って、下の英文を書き換えてみましょう。

1. They canceled all flights because of the big typhoon.
   [all flights を主語にして内容を伝える。]

   [　　　　　　　　　　　　　　　　　　　　　　　　　　　　　　　　　　　]

2. The TV station was recording the president's speech at the ceremony.
   [the president's speech を主語にして内容を伝える。]

   [　　　　　　　　　　　　　　　　　　　　　　　　　　　　　　　　　　　]

3. They have made Jimmy return the money.
   [Jimmy を主語にして内容を伝える。]

   [　　　　　　　　　　　　　　　　　　　　　　　　　　　　　　　　　　　]

4. The teacher forced the children to be quiet.
   [made を使い、同じ意味を伝える。]

   [　　　　　　　　　　　　　　　　　　　　　　　　　　　　　　　　　　　]

5. My brother is using the car right now.
   [the car を主語にして内容を伝える。]

   [   ]

Express Yourself

＜比較・対照して説明する＞

ここでは 2 つの事柄を比較して、相違点を説明する方法について練習します。

Tips:
1. 何について比較・対照するかをまず考えます。（Topic）
2. 2 つのものをどの点について比較するかを考えます。（Points of comparison）
3. それぞれの比較する点の類似点、あるいは相違点を列挙します。(Details)
4. 初めに比較 / 対照表を作るとよいでしょう。（Comprehension のキャンパスライフの表を参考にしましょう。）

比較 / 対照表：

（何について比較するか）Topic：		
比較する点	A:	B:
Subtopic 1:		
Subtopic 2:		
Subtopic 3:		

Let's Try!

Speaking Task:

1. グループで、下からトピックを一つ選び、類似点、相違点について英語で話し合い、上の比較 / 対照表を完成させましょう。
2. 比較 / 対照表をもとに、比較した内容とその類似点 / 相違点をクラスに英語で発表しましょう。

Topics:
- two different cities
- high school and university
- two sightseeing spots
- others

Writing Task:

クラスに報告した内容を、英語にしましょう。書く際は以下の順番で書きましょう。

1. 何について比較するかを述べる。
2. 比較する点とその内容について説明する。
3. 比較した内容を簡潔にまとめ、コメントをつける。

CAN-DO Check

☑ 日本とアメリカの大学生活の違いについて理解することができ　⑤　④　③　②　①
ましたか？

☑ ものごとを比較・対照して説明することができましたか？　⑤　④　③　②　①

Warm-up Questions – Talk in pairs!

1. How does weather affect your feelings and thoughts?

2. How does weather affect your daily activities?

▶ Keywords

Weather Vocabulary

Nouns	Adjectives	Related Words
sun	sunny	sunlight
rain	rainy	rainbow
wind	windy	windstorm
snow	snowy	snowflake

Conversation

Haruki and Katie are at a museum looking at a painting.

Haruki: What do you think of this painting, Katie?

Katie: I think the two people in the painting are having a serious conversation.

Haruki: What do you mean?

Katie: Well, the two faces are looking at each other as they are talking.

Haruki: What faces? This is a painting of a vase, isn't it?

Katie: Ah, I see! You're looking at the middle of painting.

Haruki: Now I see the faces on the sides! It's interesting how people can see different things in the same image.

Useful Expressions

What do you think of ...?
What do you mean?
... isn't it?

Pronunciation

イントネーション 3

This is a painting of a vase, <u>isn't it?</u> の下線部の抑揚は、上がる場合と下がる場合があります。話者の確信の度合いにより使い分け、自信がなければ上げ、確信があり同意がほしい場合は下げます。イントネーションを手掛かりに 話者の確信の度合いを聞きとる練習をしましょう。

 Let's Try!

英文を聞いて、確信があるか (sure)、確信がないか (unsure) を聞き取りましょう。

1. This is a painting of a vase, <u>isn't it?</u> (sure / unsure)

2-19

2. This is a painting of a vase, <u>isn't it?</u> (sure / unsure)

2-20

Reading

Scandinavian countries such as Iceland, Norway, Finland, Sweden, and Denmark are leading the world in creating sustainable societies. Olafur Eliasson is an Icelandic-Danish artist who was born on February 5th, 1967 in Copenhagen, Denmark. Eliasson cares deeply about the environment, and this shows in his artwork. He often designs large sculptures and *art installations using natural elements such as air, light, and water. He became a *Goodwill Ambassador for the United Nations Development Programme in 2019, working on issues such as climate change and the SDGs.

Eliasson's art projects are admired by people all over the world for their uniqueness and creativity. The viewer is often encouraged to think about the relationship between humans and nature. For example, an art installation titled "Beauty" used mist and light to create a *shimmering rainbow in a dark room. Viewers were encouraged to walk around or through the mist, interacting with the water and light. The shapes and colors of the rainbow changed depending on the position of the viewer in the room. Many people left the exhibition with the feeling that nature is both powerful and *fragile.

His art often combines art and science in innovative ways. One of his most famous art installations was "The Weather Project" at the Tate Modern art gallery in London. He put a huge mirror on the ceiling of a large open space called Turbine Hall. Then, he installed a bright light in the shape of a half-circle. Reflected in the mirror above, the light became a circle that looked like the sun. Visitors in the hall could see their own reflections on the ceiling as distant black shadows in the yellow-orange light. This made them feel small next to the beauty and power of the "sunlight." The exhibition was popular, and the art gallery reported over two million visitors in six months. Johnathan Jones, a British art critic, called Eliasson "one of the century's most significant artists."

2-24

Another one of his projects, "Ice Watch," raised awareness of climate change. He collected huge ice blocks floating in *a fjord in Greenland and transported them to several European cities. The ice blocks were arranged in public places where anyone could see them, touch them, and watch them melt away. He did this in Copenhagen in 2014, Paris in 2015, and London in 2018. The public had various opinions about this art series, which sparked conversations about climate change and the need for action. 35

2-25

In an interview, Eliasson said, "I believe art is about reflecting on the world and essentially also bringing the world forward by creating a positive vision for the future, a tomorrow, which is better than yesterday." He says that he is hopeful for the future: "Clearly the world is changing and there are huge issues that need to be solved... but I also think it's important not to 40 lose sight of what is actually going quite well. There is reason for hope."

Vocabulary

(art) installations：絵画・彫刻・映像・写真などと並ぶ現代美術における表現ジャンルの一つ。ある特定の室内や屋外などにオブジェや装置を置いて、作家の意向に沿って空間を構成し変化させ、場所や空間全体を作品として体験させる芸術。
Goodwill Ambassador：親善大使　**shimmering rainbow**：きらめく虹　**fragile**：壊れやすい　**fjord**：フィヨルド（氷河の浸食作用でできた地形）

Comprehension

Read the passage, and fill in the table below.
オラファー・エリアソンの作品について、以下の表にまとめてみましょう。

Olafur Eliasson's Art Installations	Description	Impact on People
Beauty 	Eliasson used (　　　) and (　　　) to create a shimmering rainbow in a dark room.	
	Viewers were encouraged to walk around or through the mist, interacting with the water and light. The shapes and colors of the rainbow changed depending on the (　　　) of the viewer in the room.	People feel that nature is both (　　　) and (　　　).

The Weather Project 	Eliasson put a huge ( ) on the ceiling of a large open space called Turbine Hall. Then, he installed a bright ( ) in the shape of a half-circle. Reflected in the mirror above, the light became a ( ) that looked like the ( ).	People feel that they are ( ) next to the beauty and power of the "( )."
	Visitors in the hall could see their own reflections on the ceiling as distant black shadows in the yellow-orange light.	
Ice Watch 	Eliasson collected huge ( ) ( ) floating in a fjord in Greenland and transported them to several European cities. The ice blocks were arranged in public places.	People had various opinions about this art series, which sparked ( ) about climate change and the need for ( ).
	People could see them, touch them, and watch them ( ) away.	

Answer the Questions

Work with a partner to answer the questions. Use complete sentences.

1. How does Olafur Eliasson design his artwork?

   ....

2. What do Eliasson's art projects encourage the viewers think about?

   ....

3. How many people visited Turbine Hall to see "The Weather Project" in six months?

   ....

4. After people saw "Ice Watch," what did they talk about?

   ....

5. According to Eliasson, what is important for us to do?

   ....

Discussion Topic

Does art play an important
role in your life? How
does it affect your life?

Retelling

次の表内のキーワードを参考に、「オラファー・エリアソンの作品」について英語で説明してみましょう。

Olafur Eliasson's Art Installations	Keywords
Beauty	mist / light / a shimmering rainbow / dark room / viewers / walk around or through the mist / interact / the water and light / the shapes and colors of the rainbow / the position / / the viewer in the room / nature / powerful / fragile
The Weather Project	a huge mirror / the ceiling of a large open space / Turbine Hall / a bright light / the shape / half-circle / reflect / the mirror above / the light / a circle / sun / small / visitors / the hall / reflections / the ceiling / distant black shadows / yellow-orange light / the beauty and power of the "sunlight"
Ice Watch	huge ice blocks / a fjord in Greenland / transported / several European cities / arranged / public places / people / see / touch / watch / melt away / sparked conversations / climate change / the need for action

Grammar for Communication

【情報を加えて説明する表現：関係詞①】

◆ 関係代名詞：ある名詞（句）を修飾して、情報を加えます。修飾される名詞（句）は先行詞と呼ばれます。文の中での関係代名詞の役割により、主格、目的格、所有格の形になります。

Do you know the man who is talking to Charlotte? **(主格)**

（シャーロットに話しかけている男性を知っていますか？）

I've already read the book (that) Tom gave me yesterday. **(目的格)**

（私は、トムが私に昨日くれた本をもう読んでしまいました。）

I have a friend whose father is a doctor. **(所有格)**

（私には父親が医者の友人がいます。）

＊関係代名詞の、主格、所有格、目的格には、先行詞が人の場合、who, whose, who/whom が、先行詞が物の場合は that/which, of which/whose, that/which が使われます。

◆ 関係詞には、制限用法と非制限用法があり、制限用法は先行詞の意味を限定します。一方、非制限用法は先行詞に付加的な情報をつけ足します。

★動画で分かる！
文法解説

My brother who lives in Osaka is an architect.

（大阪に住んでいる私の兄は建築家です。）

My brother, who lives in Osaka, is an architect.

（私の兄は、大阪に住んでいますが、建築家です。）

Let's Try!

下線部の名詞に（　　）の中の情報を関係詞を使って付け足しましょう。

1. The car broke down. (My father bought the car.)

   [   ]

2. The child was taken to the hospital. (The child was injured in the car accident.)

   [   ]

3. Asakusa is in the downtown area of Tokyo. (It is a popular sightseeing spot for tourists from overseas.)

   [   ]

4. There is a sign at the door. (It says "No Entry.")

   [   ]

5. J.R.R. Tolkien was a British writer. (J.R.R. Tolkien's famous works include "The Hobbit" and "The Lord of the Rings".)

   [   ]

Express Yourself

＜人物の説明をする＞

人物の説明をする練習を行います。

人物を説明する場合は次のようなことを考えて説明しましょう。

Tips:

1. いつ、どのようにしてその人を知ったか。
2. その人物とどのような関係か。
3. その人物はどのような人か。
4. その人物はどのようなことをしているか（したか）。
5. その人物についてどのように思うか。

Exercise:

表の内容を表す表現を以下から選び、表に記号を書き込みましょう。

appearance	relationship	occupation	personality

a. He is easygoing.

b. She has long black hair.

c. She is my colleague.

d. He runs a restaurant.

e. He works as a math teacher.

f. She is reliable.

g. He is my cousin.

h. She wears glasses.

Speaking Task:

1. グループになり、下のトピックの中から一つ選び、グループメンバーに人物を英語で説明しましょう。

Topics:
- my best friend
- a singer / an athlete / an actor / a scientist / a writer I like
- somebody I respect
- others

2. メンバーが話している説明の要点を書きとり、説明されたこと以外で知りたいことを英語で質問しましょう。

3. グループで話し合ったことを、クラスに英語で発表しましょう。

Writing Task:

Speaking Task1 のトピックの中から一つ選び、その人物を説明する文章を英語で書きましょう。
（グループで説明した内容と、説明した後に受けた質問を参考にしましょう。）

Lesson
10

Olafur Eliasson

CAN-DO Check

☑ オラファー・エリアソンの作品が持つメッセージを理解するこ　⑤　④　③　②　①
とができましたか？

☑ 人物について説明することができましたか？　⑤　④　③　②　①

Warm-up Questions – Talk in pairs!

1. What kind of volunteer work are you interested in?

2. What benefits do you get by volunteering?

Keywords

knowledge

experience

skills

new friends

motivation

Volunteer Work

Benefits

Types

supporting children

rescuing animals

empowering women

wildlife conservation

marine conservation

Conversation

Haruki and Katie are talking before class about what they did on the weekend.

▶ 2-27

Haruki:	I went to the beach yesterday!
Katie:	Oh, did you go surfing?
Haruki:	No. I volunteered to clean up the beach.
Katie:	By yourself?
Haruki:	No way! There were about twenty volunteers. We worked together.
Katie:	What did you do there?
Haruki:	We picked up garbage and sorted recyclable items. I made some new friends!
Katie:	How nice! Can I join you next time?
Haruki:	Sure!

Useful Expressions

No way!

How nice!

Can I ...?

Pronunciation

子音 /t/ の変化に慣れよう

会話に登場する数の twenty。春樹はアメリカ式に「トゥウェニー」のように発音していますね。知っておきたい音声変化のひとつで、語中で -nt- と続くとき、/t/ を飲み込むように発音することがあります。話すスピード、個人差、地域差などにもよります。

Let's Try!

twenty の /t/ と同じ音声変化が生じている箇所にアンダーラインを引きましょう。

2-28   Internet   interesting   interview   international   intimate   painter

Reading

2-29

A few years ago, I had an opportunity to volunteer abroad, and I would like to tell you about that experience today. My name is Daiki Kojima, and I am from Hokkaido Prefecture in Japan. I went to Indonesia for my volunteer program. I was a little bit nervous because I had never left Japan before. At Jakarta's Soekarno-Hatta International Airport, I met the local staff members who were running the program. The other volunteers came from many different countries. At the time, I didn't feel confident about my English skills. I was worried that we wouldn't understand each other. 5

2-30

However, I truly wanted to get to know the volunteers and the staff. Maybe we could even become friends! I decided that I had to do my best to communicate with them. I spoke with them using my limited English skills, as well as gestures and a few Indonesian words. To my surprise, we mostly understood each other! Our team worked by building *support posts, laying bricks, and making cement. The bricks were very heavy, so it was quite a workout! When we finished for the day, I was tired and my muscles were sore. Together, our team built a house for a family in need with help and instructions from the staff. Now, I'm back in Japan, but I still talk regularly online with the friends I made from all over the world. 10

15

2-31

I believe that volunteer work has the power to bring people together. I enjoyed working with people from different places who spoke different languages. I learned to listen and pay attention to other people's ideas and perspectives. I also had some difficult experiences. For example, the weather was usually hot and humid, and we couldn't work during sudden *tropical storms. Volunteer work also taught me about my *privilege. Before I volunteered, I took my house in Japan for granted. I didn't realize 20

25

that there are many people in the world who don't have a safe, warm shelter to come home to.

    I recommend joining a volunteer program if you are interested. Overall, my experience helped me re-examine my values and grow as a

person. For example, I decided to volunteer because I wanted to "rescue" ³⁰

the local people in countries affected by poverty. However, I quickly realized something. Maybe those people don't have an Internet connection or a nearby convenience store, but they have loving families, supportive communities, and they enjoy their lives just like I do. They helped me realize what is truly important. I wanted to help them, but I found they ³⁵ also helped me.

Vocabulary
support post(s)：支柱　tropical storms：熱帯暴風雨　privilege：特権

Comprehension

Read the passage, and fill in the table below.
ボランティアプログラムを通して、筆者が体験から学んだことについて、以下の表にまとめてみましょう。

Through my experience of volunteering abroad, I learned (that)…
Volunteer work has the (　　　) to bring people (　　　).
To listen and pay attention to other people's (　　　) and (　　　).
The weather was usually hot and humid.
We couldn't work during sudden tropical storms.
I took my (　　　) in Japan for granted.
There are many people in the world who don't have a safe, warm (　　　) to come home to.
It helped me re-examine my (　　　) and grow as a person.
The local people in countries are affected by (　　　).
Local people don't have an Internet connection or a nearby convenience store, but they have loving families, supportive communities, and they enjoy their lives just like I do.
They helped me realize what is truly important.

Lesson
11

Volunteer Work

2-32

87

Answer the Questions

Work with a partner to answer the questions. Use complete sentences.

1. When Daiki Kojima went to Indonesia for his volunteer program, why did he feel nervous?

....

2. When Daiki communicated with the volunteers and the staff for the first time, how did he speak with them?

....

3. What did Daiki's volunteer team do?

....

4. What privilege did Daiki's volunteer experience teach him about?

....

5. What did the local people help Daiki realize?

....

Discussion Topic

What do you think you can
learn by doing volunteer work?

Retelling

次の例を参考に、　　　　内のキーワードを使って、「海外ボランティアをすることによって学べること」
について英語で説明してみましょう。

（例） Through the experience of volunteering abroad, I can learn that volunteer work has the power to bring people together.

Through the experience of volunteering abroad, I can learn (that)...
（例） volunteer work / the power / bring people together
listen to other people's ideas and perspectives / cannot work during sudden tropical storms
take my house in Japan for granted / many people in the world / don't have a safe, warm shelter

re-examine my values / grow as a person / the local people in countries / affect / poverty
those local people / no Internet connection / no nearby convenience store / loving families / supportive communities / enjoy their lives / realize what is truly important

Grammar for Communication

2-33

【時・場所・理由などの情報を加える表現：関係詞②】

関係副詞は、先行詞を詳しく説明をします。関係副詞には次のものがあります。

◆ when：先行詞が時を表す

I remember the day when we took the exam.

（私は私たちが試験を受けた日を覚えています。）

◆ where：先行詞が場所を表す

The town where we live is famous for seafood.

（私たちが住んでいる町はシーフードで有名です。）

◆ how：先行詞が手段・方法を表す

This is (the way / how) she made this dish.

（これが、彼女がこの料理を作った方法です。）

＊カッコ内の the way もしくは how を省略することができます。

◆ why：先行詞が reason の場合に使われます。

We don't know the reason (why) Kent didn't come to the party.

（Kent がパーティーに来なかった理由を私たちは知りません。）

＊ the reason もしくは why を省略することができます。

関係代名詞 what

◆ what：the thing which となるものの代わりに使われます。先行詞は必要ありません。

I couldn't understand what the professor explained.

（私は教授が説明したことが理解できませんでした。）

＊ when, where, how も先行詞がなくても使うことができます。

★動画で分かる！
文法解説

Let's Try!

（　　）の中に when, where, how, why, what のいずれかを入れて文を完成させましょう。

1. I want to know the reason (　　　) the festival was canceled.

2. Let me know (　　　) you have in your bag.

3. This is the time (　　　) we left the office.

4. This is the hotel (　　　) the singer is staying.

5. I don't know (　　　) we can log in the computer.

Express Yourself

＜順番を説明する＞
順番を説明する方法を学びます。

Tips:

1. 初めに何について説明するかを述べます。
2. First, Second, Third, Finally などの順番を表す言葉を使用し、順番に手順を述べます。
3. 最後にもう一度、手順を簡単にまとめ、コメントをします。

Exercise:

以下の英文 a ～ f を並べ替えて手順を説明する文章にしましょう。

(　　1　　).

(　　2　　).

(　　3　　), and put it in the pan.

Fry it for about 3 minutes, (　　4　　).

(　　5　　).

(　　6　　).

a. It is really easy to make a sunny-side up egg, even for beginners
b. Finally, take it out onto a plate
c. These are instructions for how to make a sunny-side up egg
d. Then, break an egg open
e. First, pour some oil into the pan
f. then sprinkle salt and pepper on it

Let's Try!

Speaking Task:

次のトピックから一つ選び、グループの他のメンバーに手順を英語で説明しましょう。

Topics:
- how to cook your favorite dish
- how to go to your university from your home
- how to register for classes (explanation for first-year students)
- others

Writing Task:

Speaking Task のトピックから一つ選び、手順を説明する文章を英語で書きましょう。

CAN-DO Check

☑ ボランティア活動を行う意義について理解することができまし   ⑤   ④   ③   ②   ①
たか？

☑ ものごとの手順を順序立てて説明することができましたか？   ⑤   ④   ③   ②   ①

Lesson 12 Career

CAN-DO

☑ さまざまな職業選択の方法があることを理解し、自分ごととして考えることができる。

☑ 履歴書を英語で作成することができる。

Warm-up Questions – Talk in pairs!

1. What kinds of jobs interest you most and least?

2. What skills and qualifications are required to get a job?

Keywords

skills

communication

teamwork

problem-solving

leadership

analysis

Conversation

Professor Jones teaches a journalism class at the college. He is Katie's advisor, and she is asking him for advice.

Katie:	I'm thinking about my future career. How did you decide to become a professor?
Professor Jones:	Let me tell you about my experience. Actually, ten years ago, I wasn't interested in teaching.
Katie:	Really?
Professor Jones:	At first, I wanted to be a journalist because I wanted to learn more about the world. However, I found that my passion was inspiring people to learn more about the world. That's why I became a professor.
Katie:	That's great! You always inspire me.

Useful Expressions

At first

However

That's why ....

Pronunciation

カタカナ読みの「キャリア」に注意

「キャリア」は、職歴や経歴を意味する career と、運ぶ人（または器具）を意味する carrier の 2 種類の英単語がもとになっています。一般的なカタカナ読みの「キャリア」はキャの部分にアクセントがあるため、carrier に近い響きとなります。職歴を意味する場合、口を閉じ気味の「カ」ではじめ「リ」にアクセントをつけて「リァー」と言うと通じやすくなります。

Let's Try!

聞こえた単語に丸をつけましょう。

1. career / carrier   2. career / carrier   3. career / carrier

Reading

2-36

This article is for college students thinking about your future careers. My name is Hina Matsuda, and I am a writer. Right now, I am working on research for several articles to be published in an online newspaper. However, I didn't always dream of being a writer. How did I end up here? Let me tell you the story. 5

2-37

When I was a college student, I didn't have any particular goals or dreams. I didn't really know what I was interested in or what I wanted to do in the future. In my junior year, all of my classmates started doing self-evaluations, signing up for internships, and writing job application forms. I didn't start right away because the process seemed confusing and 10 difficult. I wish someone had explained it to me at the time. Now, I am telling you. Ask your professors or advisors for information. I especially recommend doing a self-evaluation and brushing up your English skills. You won't regret it!

2-38

When I graduated from college, I started working at a small local 15 bookstore. One of my co-workers was a young man named Sho. He had gotten a job at a bank, worked there for one year, and quit. The job paid well, but he didn't enjoy repetitive tasks like counting money. While we were working at the bookstore, he took an interest in English books. He also liked to work with children, so he decided to become an English 20 teacher. Now, he loves his job, and he makes a difference in kids' lives. Working at the bookstore wasn't his dream job, but in a way, it led to his dream job.

2-39

Of course, everyone's personality is different. For example, I have another friend, Samantha, who loves working at the bank. She is happy to 25 use her accounting skills, and enjoys helping people make financial decisions.

2-40

As for me, I still couldn't decide what I wanted to do. After about a year, I became an assistant manager at the bookstore. One day, a woman wearing a suit came in. She was a reporter for a local newspaper. She told me that she was researching an article about how large online *retailers were affecting local bookstores, and she wanted my opinion. She gave me a list of interview questions, and later, I sent her my answers in an email. 30

2-41

I received a reply from her the very next day: "Thank you for your thoughtful answers! I found them very *insightful. Would you consider 35 writing an article about this topic for our newspaper?" I agreed, and to my surprise, the article was *well-received! I was asked to write more articles, and eventually I was so busy that I quit my job at the bookstore. Today, I find my job as a writer challenging and rewarding.

2-42

I realized that your dream job isn't always something you decide, but 40 something you discover *along the way. I would recommend starting with a job generally related to your interests (for example, I started working at a bookstore because I like to read). Remember to keep an open mind and watch for new and interesting opportunities. Perhaps, like me, you'll find a fulfilling career that you never expected. 45

Lesson
12

Career

Vocabulary

retailers：小売業者　insightful：洞察力のある　well-received：好評である　along the way：進んでいくうちに

Comprehension

Read the passage, and fill in the table below.
本文の内容を参考に、筆者の進路アドバイスを以下の表にまとめてみましょう。

Suggestions for Your Future Job / Dream
- Ask your (　　　) or (　　　) for information.
- Do a (　　　).
- Brush up your (　　　) skills.
- Start with a job generally related to your (　　　).
- Remember to keep an open (　　　) and watch for (　　　) and (　　　) opportunities.

Answer the Questions

Work with a partner to answer the questions. Use complete sentences.

1. When Hina was in her junior year, what was her wish?

   ....

2. Why did one of Hina's friends, Sho, quit his job after working at a bank for a year?

   ....

3. What made Sho decide to become an English teacher?

   ....

4. Why does Hina's friend Samantha love working at the bank?

   ....

5. What did Hina realize about dream jobs?

   ....

Discussion Topic

How do you think you can
find your dream job?

Retelling

次のイラストとキーワードを使って、主人公（Hina）について、書き出しの英語に続くように英語で説明してみましょう。また、本文の内容を参考に、最後に進路に迷っている人に英語でアドバイスをしてみましょう。

a college student	graduated / college	After about a year	If you don't have any particular goals or dreams
have no particular goals or dreams	work / a small local bookstore	an assistant manager / the bookstore	you should ...

When Hina was a college student, she didn't have any particular goals or dreams.

Hina advises you that if you don't have any particular goals or dreams, you should   .

Grammar for Communication

【言葉に情報を加える表現：形容詞用法】

2-43 関係詞節を形容詞句に書き換えて、同じ意味を伝えることができます。書き換えには次のような方法があります。

◆ 現在分詞（〜ing）

The number of people <u>who wish</u> to enter the university has been increasing these days. （その大学に入学を希望する人の数が、このところ増えてきています。）

⇨ The number of people <u>wishing</u> to enter the university has been increasing these days.

◆ 過去分詞（〜ed）

The view <u>which is seen</u> through the window in this room is very beautiful.

（この部屋の窓から見る景色はとても素晴らしい。）

⇨ The view <u>seen</u> through the window in this room is very beautiful.

◆ 不定詞

I have letters which I have to read. （私が読まなければならない手紙があります。）

⇨ I have letters to read.

＊ where to (do), how to (do), when to (do), what to (do) などの
表現にも注意しましょう。

★動画で分かる！
文法解説

次の英文の関係詞節を形容詞句に書き換えてみましょう。

1. There is a security guard who is standing at the gate.

   [   ]

2. I saw a person who was running in the park.

   [   ]

3. This is a photo which was taken by my grandfather.

   [   ]

4. This is the way I change the volume of the TV.

   [   ]

5. We don't know where we should go.

   [   ]

Express Yourself

＜自分の経歴を説明する＞

自分の経歴を説明する方法を学びます。以下では、就職活動の際に自分自身について説明する場合について学びます。

Tips:

1. これまでの自分の経歴（学歴、職歴など）を英語で説明できるようにしましょう。
2. それぞれの経歴の中で特筆すべき事柄について、より詳しく説明できるようにしましょう。
3. 自分がどのような人物かを説明できるようにしましょう。

   ＊ Lesson 1 の「自己紹介をする」で学んだ Tips も参考にしましょう。

Exercise

(1)〜(7)の質問文に対する答えとなるように、a 〜 g の選択肢から適切なものを組み合わせて線で結んでみましょう。

(1) What is your name? •   • a. I am Kenichi Yoshida.

(2) What do you want to do in our company? •   • b. My biggest strength is that I can work under a lot of pressure.

(3) Do you have any special skills? •   • c. I have worked as a volunteer at an animal shelter.

(4) Tell me about any work experience. •   • d. I want to work in the sales department.

(5) What do you study at the university? •   • e. I am studying economics.

(6) Have you ever done any volunteer work? •   • f. I have advanced skills in Word and Excel.

(7) What is your greatest strength? •   • g. I have worked part-time at McDonald's.

Let's Try!

Writing Task:

下の項目に沿って、自分の履歴書（CV）を英語で作成しましょう。

CV

Personal Data（個人情報）

● 名前、住所、電話番号、e-mail のアドレスなどを記載します。

（住所を書く際は、日本語と逆の順番（番地、町名、市町村、都道府県、郵便番号の順番）になります。）

Objectives（希望職種）

● 希望の職種とそれを選んだ理由を 2 ～ 3 行程度で述べます。

Qualifications（資格）

● 資格や能力を箇条書きで書きます。

（例）Advanced user of Word, Excel and PowerPoint.

Work Experience（職歴）

● 仕事の経験（アルバイト経験など）を期間とともに箇条書きにします。

（例）20XX- Present
　　　Cashier at XX Supermarket

Education（学歴）

● 学歴を現在から過去にさかのぼって書きます。

● 取得した学位を書きます。

　（例）　20XX- 20XX　〇〇 University
　　　　　B.A. in ～（～には専攻が入ります）

Activities（活動）

● 今まで行ってきた、部活動、ボランティア、ゼミなどでの役割について書きます。

● 企業と関連のある活動について記載します。

Speaking Task:

①ペアになり、就職の面接のロールプレイを行いましょう。

　A：仕事の面接官になり、面接をします。CV のそれぞれの項目について英語で質問をしましょう。

　B：面接を受ける人になり、相手の質問に英語で答えましょう。

②終わったら役割を交代しましょう。

CAN-DO Check

☑ さまざまな職業選択の方法があることを理解し、自分ごととして考えることができましたか？　　　　⑤　④　③　②　①

☑ 履歴書を英語で作成することができましたか？　　　　⑤　④　③　②　①

Lesson 13 Travel

CAN-DO

☑ 交通手段が発達してきた歴史を理解することができる。

☑ 場所について説明することができる。

Warm-up Questions – Talk in pairs!

1. Do you prefer to travel by car or train?

2. How many different kinds of transportation have you been on?

Keywords

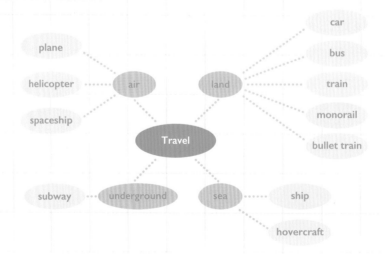

Conversation

Katie tells Haruki about a presentation that will happen on campus that week. The woman giving the presentation arrived that day on a flight from Tokyo.

Katie: Haruki, have you heard? On Wednesday, a woman named Janet Smith is going to give a presentation about living in the U.S. and Japan. She's a graduate of this college.

Haruki: That sounds interesting!

Katie: Yes. I was going to interview her this evening, but I was told that she went to bed already.

Haruki: Really? It's only six thirty!

Katie: I guess she has jet lag. She just traveled about halfway around the world!

Useful Expressions

Have you heard?

Really?

I guess ….

Pronunciation

数字の読み方

この本文では、年号や年代などの数字がいくつか登場します。発音の仕方をおさえておきましょう。
1998 年や 2016 年は、"nineteen ninety-eight"、"twenty sixteen" のように 2 桁ずつ読みます。
1903 年のように 10 の位に 0 が入る時は「0」を「オゥ」と読み "nineteen-o-three" と発音します。
1900 年は "nineteen hundred" です。ホテルの部屋番号や飛行機の便名などで 3 桁のものは、例えば Room 315 を "three fifteen" のように読みます。

Let's Try!

本文中に登場した数字を聞いて書き取りましょう。

1. _____ 2. _____ 3. _____ 4. _____
5. _____ 6. _____ 7. _____ 8. _____

Reading

For most of human history, it took months or even years to travel long distances. Long trips were dangerous and expensive, so long-distance travel was not common. Now, these distances can be *traversed in a matter of hours or days. This change was brought about by technological advances in transportation, including vehicles such as automobiles and airplanes. 5

The invention of the automobile was a great advance in transportation. Since the 1700s, people had been experimenting with vehicles that could carry passengers. Karl Benz was a German engineer who invented the first automobile with an *internal-combustion engine. In 1886, he received a *patent for his automobile, the Benz Patent Motorwagen. In 1888, it 10 became the first commercially available automobile. His wife and business partner, Bertha Benz, wanted to prove that it could drive long distances. Without telling her husband of her plan, she drove over one hundred kilometers in one day, stopping several times along the way to make repairs and improve the vehicle. In modern Germany, the route that she took is 15 called the Bertha Benz Memorial Route. This achievement is considered the first long-distance automobile trip.

The airplane was another important advance in technology. Even in ancient Greece, humans had experimented with flight. However, the first "sustained and controlled heavier-than-air powered flight" was achieved by 20 the Wright brothers, Orville and Wilbur Wright, in the United States in 1903. For their first successful flight, Orville flew about 120 feet in twelve seconds. After a few more tries, Wilbur managed to fly 852 feet in fifty-nine seconds. After these *groundbreaking achievements, airplane technology advanced very quickly. The first jet airliner, the Boeing 707, 25 was introduced by Boeing Commercial Airplanes in 1958. It could carry over one hundred passengers, and it could travel thousands of kilometers. Its *wingspan was about 130 feet, longer than the distance of Orville Wright's first flight. In less than one hundred years, flight technology had changed dramatically. 30

2-49

What is the next step in transportation technology? Some might argue that it will be space travel or "spaceflight." Maybe someday, humans will travel to other planets as easily as they travel to other countries. The first Moon landing was in 1969, yet humans have not visited any other celestial bodies so far. However, unmanned spacecraft can go incredible distances, 35 even beyond our solar system. Perhaps one day, people will be able to travel those distances as well.

Vocabulary
traverse：横断する internal-combustion engine：内燃機関エンジン（ガソリン等の燃料を混合気として燃焼させ、その圧力を利用して動力を得るエンジン） patent：特許 groundbreaking：草分けの wingspan：（航空機・鳥などの）両翼の端から端までの長さ

Comprehension

Read the passage, and fill in the table below.
本文に書かれている、乗り物の情報を以下の表にまとめてみましょう。

Time	Technological advances in transportation
	AUTOMOBILES
	The Benz Motorwagen was invented by ( ), a German engineer.
	It was the first automobile with an internal-combustion engine.
1886	Benz received a ( ) for his automobile.
1888	It became the first ( ) ( ) automobile.
	Bertha Benz, Karl's wife and business partner, wanted to prove that it could drive ( ) ( ).

AIRPLANES		
1903	The first sustained and controlled heavier-than-air powered flight was achieved by the ( ) ( ) in the United States.	
	Orville succeeded in the ( ) ( ), and he flew about 120 feet in twelve seconds.	
	Wilbur managed to fly ( ) feet in ( ) seconds.	
1958	The Boeing 707, the first jet airliner, was introduced by Boeing Commercial Airplanes. It could ( ) over one hundred passengers, and could ( ) thousands of kilometers. Its ( ) was about 130 feet, longer than the distance of Orville Wright's first flight.	

Answer the Questions

Work with a partner to answer the questions. Use complete sentences.

1. What kind of automobile did Karl Benz invent?

   ....

2. What did Bertha Benz do without telling Karl about her plan?

   ....

3. What is the name of the route that Bertha Benz took in Germany?

   ....

4. What did people in ancient Greece experiment with?

   ....

5. What is one thing that humans have not achieved?

   ....

Discussion Topic

Do you want to travel to other planets?
Why? / Why not?

Retelling

「宇宙旅行」について、次のイラストとキーワードを参考に、英語で説明してみましょう。

Maybe someday, humans will...

travel to other planets

travel to other countries

beyond the solar system

incredible distance

easily

Maybe someday,   .

The first Moon landing was in 1969, yet humans have not visited any other

celestial bodies so far. However,

         .

Perhaps one day, people will be able to travel those distances as well.

Grammar for Communication

▶
2-50

【自分の願いを伝える表現：仮定法】

仮定の話を述べるには次のようなものがあります。

◆ **仮定法過去**：現在の事実と異なる仮定を表す。
- might/would/could/should ＋ 動詞　で表します。「～かもしれない / ～だろう / ～できる のに / ～したほうがよい」という意味を表します。
- 「もし～ならば」という意味の if 節をつける場合には、if 節中では動詞の過去形を使います。

If he was/were here, I could ask him about the party. （もし彼がここにいれば彼に パーティーのことを聞けるのですが。）

◆ **仮定法過去完了**：過去の事実と異なる仮定を表します。
- might/would/could/should ＋ have ＋ 過去分詞で表します。「～だったかもしれない / ～ だっただろう / ～できたのに / ～すべきだった」という意味を表します。
- 「もし～だったらば」という意味の if 節をつける場合は、if 節中では「had ＋ 過去分詞」を使います。

He would have been here if you had called him. （もしあなたが彼に電話をしていたら、 彼はここにいたのに。）

★動画で分かる！
文法解説

◆ I wish 主語 ＋ 動詞の過去形 /might/would/could/should ＋ 動詞)
- 現在の事実とは異なる願望を表します。「～だったらなあ」「～できたらいいの に」という意味を表します。

I wish my friends could come with me. （友達も私と一緒に来られればいいのに。）

仮定法を使って英文を書き換えてみましょう。※（　）内に指示があるものはそれに従って書き変えましょう。

例：He got to the station in time to catch the train.

［答え：If he had not gotten to the station in time, he couldn't/wouldn't have caught the train.］

1. I want to email my friend, but I don't know his email address.

   [   ]

2. I don't have my wallet with me, so I can't buy this book.

   [   ]

3. I can't go to the theater, but I'd love to.（I wish で始まる文にする）

   [   ]

4. Tim wasn't injured in the car accident because he was wearing a seatbelt.

   [   ]

5. I regret that I never learned to play the piano in my childhood.

   [   ]

Express Yourself

＜場所を説明する＞

場所について説明をする方法を学びます。場所を説明する際には次のような点に気をつけましょう。

Tips:

1. その場所がどこにあるのかを説明しましょう。
2. その場所がどのような特徴があるかを説明しましょう。

Exercise:

　　　　　　の語（句）から空所に入るものを選び、適切な形に変えて、空所を埋めて英文を完成させましょう。

1. Edinburgh is .... of Scotland, the UK.

2. Thailand is .... in the tropical zone.

3. Akihabara is one of the most popular .... in Tokyo.

4. We can see the top of the mountain .... with snow in winter.

5. The landscape is really ....

6. The public transportation in Tokyo is well ...., so you can easily travel without a car.

Lesson

13

Travel

the capital city   sightseeing spots   locate
develop   cover   photogenic

Let's Try!

Speaking Task:

グループで好きな都市を選んで、特徴、観光スポット、おすすめなどを話し合い、選んだ都市についてどのようなところかをクラスに英語で説明しましょう。

Writing Task:

自分の hometown を紹介する文章を英語で書きましょう。

CAN-DO Check

☑ 交通手段が発達してきた歴史を理解することができましたか？　　⑤　④　③　②　①

☑ 場所について説明することができましたか？　　⑤　④　③　②　①

Warm-up Questions – Talk in pairs!

1. What do you like about your culture? / What don't you like about your culture?

2. What is considered rude in your culture?

▶ Keywords

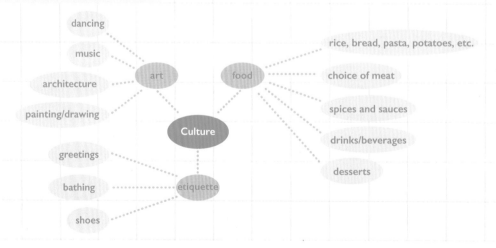

Conversation

Katie shows Haruki a magazine article about an event at their college on Wednesday evening.

2-51

Katie: Haruki, let's go to this event on Wednesday. Janet Smith is going to give a talk.

Haruki: What is she going to talk about?

Katie: About her experience living in the United States and Japan. I think you can relate to her experience!

Haruki: That sounds interesting.

Katie: There will be a reception after her talk. I want to ask her some questions for the school newspaper.

Haruki: OK, let's go together!

Useful Expressions

Let's go to ....
That sounds interesting.
OK, let's go together!

Pronunciation

促音（小さい「ッ」）は英語にない

英単語をカタカナで書く場合、「レッツゴー！」のように促音（＝小さい「ッ」）をよく使いますが、実は英語に促音はありません。"Let's" は「レッツ」と言うより「レ」と言った後に "ts" を軽く添えるように発音した方が英語らしく響きます。人名の "Janet" も「ジャネット」と書きますが、「ジャーニ t」のように発音します。

Reading

2-52

Hello, everyone. Thank you so much for coming to my talk this evening. My name is Janet Smith, and I am going to talk about my experiences living in the United States and in Japan. I studied Japanese at this college more than ten years ago. In my sophomore year of college, I visited Japan for the first time. I stayed in Tokyo for only one week, but I knew right away that I wanted to come again. My chance came in my junior year, when I decided to study abroad in Tokyo. 5

2-53

I was very lucky to be able to study in Tokyo for six months. I lived with a host family, an older couple named Mr. and Mrs. Hara. They introduced me to daily life in a Japanese home. Of course, many small cultural differences were surprising and sometimes frustrating. I forgot to take off my shoes in the house, and I forgot to change my slippers in the bathroom. I was startled to learn that the family used the same water to take a bath in the evening. I was confused when my host mother offered me more and more to eat, and often I had to say "no" many times before she would agree. These differences may seem small, but they made me feel *awkward and out-of-place. 10

15

2-54

Slowly, I started to get used to life in Japan. Things that had surprised me before began to seem ordinary. After I graduated from college in the U.S., I decided to go back to Japan as an English teacher. Now, I have lived in Tokyo for about ten years. Some things still seem different and confusing, but I am able to lead a life that I love. 20

2-55

Then, last year, I got an urgent phone call from my mother. My parents were retired and living in Florida. I heard that my father had been *diagnosed with cancer, and my mother needed help to take care of him. 25

So, I went to the U.S. to live with my parents for five months. Thankfully, my father is now in good health. He says that he was able to get better because of the support from my mother and me.

2-56

I realized something very interesting when I was living in the U.S. I experienced "reverse culture shock." Things that had seemed ordinary to me before now seemed strange. I was surprised when my parents didn't take off their shoes in the house. Their house had a shower in the bathroom, but it didn't have a bathtub. I had to practice driving a car again after so many years riding the Tokyo trains. I was shocked to feel awkward and out-of-place in the country where I had grown up.

2-57

At first, I felt frustrated, but now I realize what an amazing experience I had. Now, both Japanese and American culture seem fresh and exciting to me, but they also feel comfortable and familiar. I love my daily life in Tokyo, but I also enjoy my time spent in the United States. I realize that my experience in two cultures has changed me in many ways. If you have a chance, I recommend living abroad, even for a short while. I promise that you will find out something new about yourself.

> **Vocabulary**
> awkward：落ち着かない・居心地が悪い　be diagnosed with [A]：[A] と診断される

Comprehension

Read the passage, and fill in the table below.
ジャネットが体験したカルチャーショックを以下の表にまとめてみましょう。

Time	Cultural Differences Janet Experienced
When Janet studied in Japan	She forgot to (　　　　　) (　　　　　) her shoes in the house.
	She forgot to (　　　　　) her slippers in the bathroom.
	Her host family used the (　　　　　) water to take a bath in the evening.
	Her host mother offered her more and more to eat.
	She had to say "(　　　　　)" many times before her host mother would agree.

III

Last year, when Janet was living in the U.S.	Her parents ( ) ( ) ( ) their shoes in the house.
	Their house had a ( ) in the bathroom, but it didn't have a bathtub.
	She had to ( ) driving a car ( ) after so many years riding the Tokyo trains.

Answer the Questions

Work with a partner to answer the questions. Use complete sentences.

1. How long did Janet stay in Tokyo when she was in her junior year?

   ....

2. Before she studied abroad, did Janet take off her shoes in the house when she was in the U.S.?

   ....

3. How did cultural differences make Janet feel?

   ....

4. What is the meaning of "reverse culture shock?"

   ....

5. Where does Janet live now?

   ....

Discussion Topic

Have you ever experienced culture shock?

Retelling

ジャネットにとって2つの国で暮らした経験によって変わったことから、どのようなアドバイスをしているかについて、次の　　　　内のキーワードとイラストを参考に、英語で説明してみましょう。

Janet's Recommendation (If you have a chance, you should....)		
live abroad	even / a short while	find out something new / yourself

Lesson
14

Culture

Janet realized that her experience in two cultures changed her in many ways. According to Janet, if you have a chance, ...

Grammar for Communication

2-58

【人の言葉を伝える表現：話法】

人（第三者）の話を伝える表現には次のようなものがあります。

◆ 直接話法：引用符（" "）を使い、相手の言った言葉をそのまま伝える。

Jimmy said, "I will go to the theater tomorrow." （Jimmy は「明日劇場に行く」と言いました。）

◆ 間接話法：聞き手 / 話し手の視点から言い換えて、他人の言った内容を伝えます。

Jimmy said, "I will go to the theater tomorrow."

➡ Jimmy said that he would go to the theater the next day.

＊引用する部分が疑問文の場合は、主節の動詞を ask などに変え、疑問文を if, whether などの節に変えます。

The man said, "Do you have any change?" （その男性は「小銭はありますか？」言いました。）

➡ The man asked if I had any change.

＊引用する部分が命令文の場合は、主節の動詞を tell などに変え、命令文を to 不定詞で表します。

My mother said to my sister, "Go to bed!" （母は妹に「寝なさい」と言いました。）

➡ My mother told my sister to go to bed.

＊ according to（〜によれば）、reportedly などを使って、間接話法を記述することもできます。

According to Jimmy, he would go to the theater the next day.

（Jimmy によると、彼はその次の日に劇場に行くそうです。）

★動画で分かる！
文法解説

Let's Try!

直接話法は間接話法に、間接話法は直接話法に書き換えてみましょう。※（　）内に指示のあるものは、それに従って書き変えましょう。

1. The teacher told his students, "Be quiet!"

[   ]

113

2. The newspaper said, "There was a big fire downtown."

[   ]

3. The woman asked the passerby, "Can you tell me how to get to the station?"

[   ]

4. My friend asked me whether she could use my notebook.

[   ]

5. It is reported that the country produces a rare metal resource. （「報道によると」という出だしで文を始める。）

[   ]

Express Yourself

＜説得をする＞
人を説得するようなスピーチやライティングの方法について学びます。
はじめに、基本となる複数のパラグラフからなる文章の構造について学びます。

＜複数のパラグラフからなる文章の構造＞
複数のパラグラフからなる文章は introduction（導入）、body（本文）、conclusion（結論）の 3 つの種類のパラグラフから構成されます。それぞれのパラグラフは次のような働きをします。

- Introduction：自分の主張をするための導入の話と、thesis statement とよばれる文章全体の内容を表す主題（自分の言いたいこと）が含まれます。
- Body：主題に関して、それをサポートする具体例、理由、主張（subtopics）が含まれます。
- Conclusion：Body で述べたことの簡単なまとめと、文章全体の内容を表す主題が含まれます。

＜説得する文章を書く / 話す＞
上記の複数のパラグラフからなる文章の構造を、人を説得する文章を書いたり、話したりする場合に当てはめると次の様になります。

- Introduction：自分の主張を述べる。
- Body：自分の主張が正しいことを支持する理由、具体例を述べる。
- Conclusion：Body で述べた点を短くまとめた上で、自分の主張をもう一度述べる。

人を説得する際には、どれだけ相手を納得させるかが重要となります。次の 3 つのうちのどれかを使うと説得力が増します。
Tips:
1. 人にとって正しい行いであるということを示す
2. 聞き手 / 読み手の感情に訴えかける
3. 事実や論理的に主張を示す

Speaking Task:

1. 「海外に住む経験をしたほうが良い」と思われる理由について、グループで英語で話し合いましょう。

2. 話し合いの結果を、下の発表フォーマットに合わせて原稿を作り、クラスに英語で発表しましょう。

＊ Introduction では「海外に住む経験をしたほうが良い」と述べましょう。

＊ Body では、よいと思う理由を3つ考えましょう。

＊ Conclusion では、Body で述べたことを短くまとめて、「海外に住む経験をしたほうが良い」ともう一度述べましょう。

発表フォーマット

Introduction	
Body：理由①	
Body：理由②	
Body：理由③	
Conclusion	

Writing Task:

「他の文化を経験したほうが良い」と説得をする文章を、発表をもとに英語で書いてみましょう。

CAN-DO Check

☑ カルチャーショックの具体例を理解することができましたか？ ⑤ ④ ③ ② ①

☑ 説得力のある文章構成で伝えることができましたか？ ⑤ ④ ③ ② ①

Lesson 15 An International World

CAN-DO

☑ 留学を通して得られることを理解することができる。

☑ 自分の意見を論理的に述べることができる。

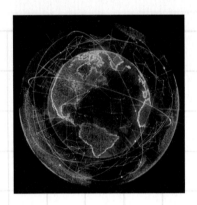

Warm-up Questions – Talk in pairs!

1. What products from other countries do you like?

2. What movies from other countries have you seen?

Keywords

Conversation

Katie and Haruki talk to Ms. Smith at the reception after her talk.

2-59

Katie:	Hello, Ms. Smith. I'm Katie. We really enjoyed your talk.
Janet:	Oh, thank you so much.
Haruki:	My name is Haruki. I'm an exchange student from Japan.
Janet:	I see!
Haruki:	I'll be going back to Japan soon. I wonder if I'll experience reverse culture shock, like you said.
Janet:	I'm sure you will. I think you'll learn something new about yourself.
Katie:	Can I ask you a few questions for the school newspaper?
Janet:	Certainly.
Haruki:	Hmm...something new about myself...

Useful Expressions

I'm sure ....

I think ....

Certainly.

Pronunciation

後ろに you が続く時

"Thank you" のように、動詞や前置詞に you か your が続く時、2 つの語をつなげて発音することが多いです。カタカナでも「サンク　ユー」ではなく「サンキュー」と 1 語のように表記しますが、これは実際の発音から 1 語のように聞こえるためです。会話では、6 〜 9 行目に① like you said、② about yourself、③ ask you とありますから、お手本をよく聞いて音のつなげ方をまねして、耳と口を鍛えましょう。

Reading

I went to an interesting talk today. A woman named Janet Smith talked about her experiences living in the United States and Japan. Her talk made me think about my own experiences. Now, I wonder how I will feel when I go back to Japan after studying in the U.S.

Ms. Smith said that she felt culture shock when she arrived in Japan for the first time. She said that everything seemed exciting but confusing. As she talked, I found myself nodding. I understood exactly what she meant. I love living in Boston, but a lot of things have seemed strange to me, too. It takes time to get used to different food, language, and customs. It has been challenging but fun.

Then, Ms. Smith said something that surprised me. She said, "You will learn something new about yourself." I had to think about that. By coming to another country, I expected to learn about another culture. I knew that I would learn about other people's language and customs. But, learn about myself? I knew everything about myself already! Or did I? Had I learned something new about myself? Would I be the same person without my experiences?

Well, I suppose that people change with every experience they have. I know the Haruki who lived in Kanagawa, who walked the same path to the station every morning, bought snacks and juice at the convenience store, and played baseball with his friends until *dusk. I also know the Haruki who lives in Boston, who walks along the *red brick sidewalks, orders *pepperoni pizza at the college cafeteria, and watches football games with friends in the chilly evening air.

10

15

20

25

2-64

I thought about it. Now, all of these experiences seem special, somehow. They are both familiar and unfamiliar. Hmm. Can something 30 be both? Maybe, like rediscovering some old photographs, or seeing a close friend who you haven't met for a long time. They're the same, but somehow different from before. Maybe they haven't changed, but you have changed. I know that it's difficult and exciting to adapt to a new culture. Maybe it's just as difficult and exciting to adapt to your own culture again. What a 35 strange idea! Who knows? When I get back to Japan, maybe I'll see it with new eyes.

広告 ビジネス プライバシー 規約 設定

Vocabulary

dusk：夕方・日暮れ　**red brick sidewalk(s)**：赤いレンガで舗装された歩道　**pepperoni pizza**：スパイスの利いたサラミ入りのトマト・チーズのピザ

Comprehension

Read the passage, and fill in the table below.

1. 春樹のブログの内容から、留学を通して得られると期待できるものを以下の表にまとめてみましょう。

By coming to another country, you can expect to learn …
· about another (　　　　)
· other people's (　　　　) and (　　　　)
· something new about (　　　　)

2. 神奈川にいた時の春樹とボストンでの春樹を比較し、以下の表にまとめてみましょう。

Haruki in Kanagawa	Haruki in Boston
walked the same (　　　　) to the (　　　　) every morning.	walks along the red brick (　　　　).
bought (　　　) and (　　　) at the (　　　) store.	orders pepperoni (　　　) at the college (　　　).
played (　　　) with his friends until (　　　).	watches (　　　) games with friends in the chilly (　　　) air.

119

Answer the Questions

Work with a partner to answer the questions. Use complete sentences.

1. Why did Ms. Smith feel culture shock when she visited Japan for the first time?

   ....

2. What was Ms. Smith's statement that made Haruki surprised?

   ....

3. Does Haruki think himself to be the same person before and after his experiences?

   ....

4. How does Haruki suppose people change?

   ....

5. What does Haruki think will be difficult and exciting when he gets back to Japan?

   ....

Discussion Topic

How do you think you will change
when you graduate from college?

Retelling

「経験することによってものの見え方が変わること」について、次の　　　　　内のキーワードとイラスト
を参考に、英語で説明してみましょう。

People change with every experience they have.			
rediscover some old photographs	see a close friend / not meet / a long time	the same / somehow different	
before		after (they haven't changed / you have changed)	

120

People change with every experience they have. Maybe it feels like ....

....

Maybe they haven't changed, but you have changed.

Grammar for Communication

【論理的に伝える表現：ディスコース標識】

2-65　話し手、あるいは書き手の伝えたい内容を論理的に示したり、文と文、パラグラフの関係性をはっきりとさせたりするために用いられる副詞（句）、接続詞、前置詞句をディスコース標識といいます。

◆ 理由を明確にする

　　because, for, as, since, so, because of, owing to など

◆ 逆接を表す

　　but, though, although, however, even so, nevertheless, yet, on the contrary など

◆ 順接を表す

　　and, of course, as you will see, obviously, clearly など

◆ 意見をまとめる

　　therefore, thus, in conclusion, as a result, to sum up など

◆ 追加する

　　what is more/worse, moreover, in addition, also など

◆ 順番を表す

　　first, second, third, finally, in the first place など

◆ 同様なものを表す

　　as well, likewise, like, similarly, in the same way など

◆ 強調する

　　above all, particularly, in particular, indeed, especially など

◆ 一般化する

　　generally, in general, on the whole など

★動画で分かる！
文法解説

Let's Try!

次の文と文の間にある（　　）の中に適切なディスコース標識を入れ、文章を完成させましょう。

1. There are many problems with the plan. (　　　) I disagreed with it.
   (　　　), most of the members agreed with it.

2. Last Sunday, I had a bad day. I left my umbrella on the train. (　　　), I had to go home in the rain. (　　　), I lost my purse. I couldn't buy anything (　　　) I was really hungry.

Express Yourself

論理的に自分の意見を述べる方法について学びましょう。

意見を述べるには次の点に注意します。

Tips:

1. 論理的、確証的な事例や、証拠を用いて自分の主張を補強する。
2. 自分の意見と反対の意見を説明し、反証する。

スピーチも、ライティングも次のようなパターンをとります。

Introduction：自分の主張を述べる。

Body：①自分の主張が正しい理由を述べる。

②自分とは反対の意見を述べて、反証する。

Conclusion：Body で主張したことを短くまとめて、改めて自分の主張を述べる。

Exercise

次の英文を、論説のパターンに合わせて適切な順番に並べ替えましょう。（答えは下の論説の
パターン表に書き入れましょう。）

a. Some people say disposable wooden chopsticks are not ecological. However, using them can lead to protection of the forest.

b. Disposable wooden chopsticks are good for the forest industry and forest preservation. Therefore, I agree with using them.

c. Second, disposable wooden chopsticks can help the forest industry.

d. I agree with using disposable wooden chopsticks at restaurants. I have two reasons for this.

e. First, disposable wooden chopsticks are good for sanitary reasons.

Introduction	
Subtopic：理由 1	
Subtopic：理由 2	
Rebuttal：反論	
Conclusion	

Speaking Task:

グループで、以下のテーマの中から一つ選び、賛成か反対かの立場を決めて、グループの意見をクラスに英語で発表しましょう。

Topics:
● using plastic straws
● using plastic bags
● using our own coffee tumbler
● others

Writing Task:

上のトピックの中から一つ選び、賛成か反対かの立場を決めて、自分の意見を英語で書いてみましょう。

CAN-DO Check

☑ 留学を通して得られることを理解することができましたか？　　⑤　④　③　②　①

☑ 自分の意見を論理的に述べることができましたか？　　⑤　④　③　②　①

グローバル社会へのコミュニケーション英語

検印
省略

© 2023年1月31日

編著者	阿野幸一
	上田倫史
	遠山道子
	豊嶋正貴
	町村貴子
	Karen Haedrich
発行者	小川洋一郎
発行所	株式会社　朝日出版社

101-0065 東京都千代田区西神田 3-3-5
電話 (03) 3239-0271
Fax (03) 3239-0479
e-mail: text-e@asahipress.com
URL http://text.asahipress.com/english
振替口座　00140-2-46008
組版・明昌堂／製版・図書印刷

乱丁、落丁本はお取替えいたします。
ISBN978-4-255-15704-7 C1082